# SEWN TOGETHER

**LARK**
New York

An Imprint of Sterling Publishing
1166 Avenue of the Americas
New York, NY 10036

ISBN 978-1-4547-0877-3

Distributed in Canada by Sterling Publishing
c/o Canadian Manda Group, 664 Annette Street
Toronto, Ontario, Canada M6S 2C8
Distributed in the United Kingdom by GMC Distribution Services
Castle Place, 166 High Street, Lewes, East Sussex, England BN7 1XU
Distributed in Australia by Capricorn Link (Australia) Pty. Ltd.
P.O. Box 704, Windsor, NSW 2756, Australia

For information about custom editions, special sales, and premium and corporate purchases,
please contact Sterling Special Sales at 800-805-5489 or specialsales@sterlingpublishing.com.

Manufactured in China

2  4  6  8  10  9  7  5  3  1

larkcrafts.com

# SEWN TOGETHER

## 25 Fun Projects to Sew with Kids

Jenny Doh

LARK

New York

# CONTENTS

# GETTING STARTED

**W**elcome to *Sewn Together*! In the pages of this creativity-filled book, you'll find project after project to work on with your favorite young sewer. The craft of sewing is meant to be shared among friends and between generations old and young, but there's an art to teaching sewing in an approachable, fun way. This book will guide you as you work together with children to create projects to wear, play with, and proudly display in your home. Before we dive in, let's talk about basic materials you'll need to have and techniques you'll need to understand in order to complete the projects in this book, with helpful tips along the way for working with young ones.

# Sewing by Hand

At its core, sewing requires a needle, thread, and something to stitch. Before we move on to working with a machine, it's key that your young ones understand the notion of hand sewing. The beauty of learning hand sewing first is that even complicated sewing machine projects can be done by hand instead. Plus, most sewing machine projects require the use of hand sewing at some point.

## Supplies

Begin by gathering your tools and materials in the Basic Hand-Sewing Tool Kit (see opposite page), details of which we will discuss below and on pages 10–11.

### NEEDLES AND THIMBLE

Needles come in an assortment of types and sizes. It's best to have a variety on hand so you can quickly choose the appropriate needle for any project, taking into consideration fabric, thread weight, and project durability needs. If you plan to try out embroidery, include a selection of needles with larger eyes. It's also a good idea to keep a thimble close, which will protect your finger when pushing a needle through fabric.

### THREAD

Thread is available in a wide range of styles to fit your hand-sewing needs. Cotton thread is ideal for light- to medium-weight fabrics that have little or no stretch to them; cotton thread doesn't have much give, so the stitches will break if used on a stretchy fabric such as knit. Polyester thread is suitable for projects that involve stretchy fabrics. Cotton-wrapped polyester is the most common thread used in sewing projects; it's an all-purpose thread that can handle all types of fabric. Other options include quilting thread, metallic thread, heavy duty thread, and silk thread, more suited for specific projects; we won't work with these threads in the projects in this book.

A good rule of thumb is to select a color of thread that matches the dominant fabric color you're working with. If you can't find an exact match, choose a color a shade or two darker; lighter shades of thread will stand out more against a darker fabric. In a similar vein, select a thread that most closely matches the fiber content of your fabric.

For the projects in this book, we'll make a note if you need to find a specific thread. In general, it's a good idea to have basic colors and styles on hand so you're ready for whatever sewing projects come your way.

### NEEDLE THREADER

When it's time to thread your needle, a needle threader can come in handy, particularly for delicate needles and threads. Simply push the wire loop of the threader through the eye of the needle, then pull one end of the thread through the loop. Pull the wire loop back through the eye of the needle, taking the thread with it, and then remove the threader.

### SCISSORS

Any good seamstress knows the value of a great, sharp pair of sewing scissors. But since we're working with kids on the projects in this book, we also need to take safety into consideration. It's important to choose a pair of scissors that are age appropriate, but sharp enough that kids will have control over cutting.

# BASIC HAND-SEWING TOOL KIT

- Needles in a variety of sizes
- Thimble
- Thread
- Needle threader
- Scissors
- Straight pins
- Pincushion or magnetic pin dish
- Seam ripper
- Marking tools*

- Pencil and eraser (for light-colored fabrics when marks don't need to be completely removed)
- Air- and water-removable fabric marker (for any color of fabric, and usually marks that are completely removable)
- Tailor's chalk (for dark-colored fabrics; usually brushes off, but depends on the type of chalk)

*Choose the marking tool most appropriate for your project. If you want to completely remove the marks, test the marker on the fabric you will be using and follow manufacturer's instructions.*

## STRAIGHT PINS AND PINCUSHION

Straight pins are a necessity in any sewing project, helping to keep fabric pieces secure as you sew and in general holding everything together. It may be helpful to provide young sewers with a set of their own pins with brightly-colored heads that are easy to see and grab. And a pincushion or magnetic pin dish is ideal for corralling those pins as you're working. As a bonus, it's also a great place to keep a few loose needles.

## SEAM RIPPER

We all make mistakes when sewing, especially when we're working with kids. A seam ripper comes in handy for removing stitches that don't belong—stitches that went an inch too far or perhaps went a little crooked. Simply place the hook of the seam ripper underneath the thread, and pull up to cut it.

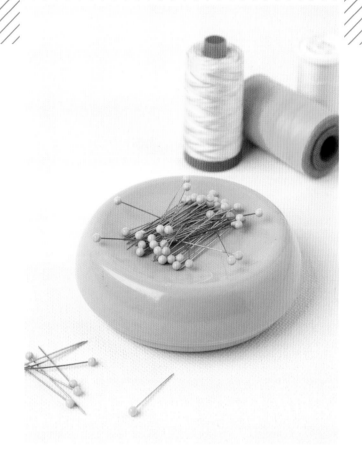

# A WORD ABOUT FABRIC

The projects in this book will include details about the fabric you'll need to complete them, so be sure to look at the materials list before beginning. Many of the projects will have you pin and sew fabric pieces together with the right sides facing each other, before turning them ride side out to finish. When teaching children about sewing with fabric, it may be helpful to explain this concept in ways they can understand; talking about the "pretty side" or the "smooth side" of the fabric will help them grasp the idea. Any necessary project templates are included in the book as well.

# Hand-Sewing Stitches

There are many different ways to thread a needle and knot the thread, and you probably already have preferences. Here are four steps that can help explain the process: 1. Cut a length of thread about 20 inches (50.8 cm) long. 2. Push the thread through the needle's eye and pull it through a ways. For doubled thread, match up the cut ends and continue; for sewing with a single strand of thread, continue with one end of the thread. 3. Form an X with the pointed end of the needle and the end(s) of the thread. With one hand, firmly pinch the thread where it crosses the needle. With the other hand, wrap the thread around the needle three times. 4. Pull the wrapped thread down the needle, over the eye, and off the needle altogether. Keep pulling until the knot reaches the end(s) of the thread.

backstitch

- A **running stitch** is created by running the needle and thread up and back down through the layer(s) of fabric. It is a great one to use in basting, to hold your fabric pieces together with loose stitches rather than pins.

slip stitch

- The **backstitch** creates a strong seam, and it's often used at the beginning and end of sewing to create a secure seam.

- A **slip stitch** is used to create an invisible seam between two folded edges; it's perfect for binding, for the final stitches on a stuffed pillow, or to close an opening.

whipstitch

- The **whipstitch** is great for finishing techniques; it has slanted stitches on the wrong side and small stitches on the right side. This stitch is used often use in this book, for finishing projects such as stuffed pillows and dolls.

herringbone stitch

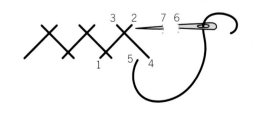

- And finally, the **herringbone stitch** gets its name from the herring fish because the stitch pattern resembles the bones from the spine of the fish.

# Hand Sewing With Kids

Before you give young sewers a sharp needle and thread, it's smart to be sure they are ready, both skill-wise and age-wise. A good place to start is by teaching them to thread a piece of yarn through a sheet of cardstock with holes punched out of it. By guiding them in the process of pushing the yarn up through the back of the cardstock, then back down through the next hole, they will gain an understanding of the basic concept of a running stitch.

After they've mastered this, children can progress to hand-sewing on fabric. With a water-soluble fabric marker, draw a guide of dots or dashes on the fabric. This will help kids see where needles can come up and re-enter fabric and will help them better understand how to space stitches properly.

Guide your young sewers in how to hold the needle and fabric so their fingers are clear of the needle. Teach them to keep the fabric taut so it doesn't pucker as they stitch, and have them keep an eye on their thread so it doesn't get tangled.

# Using a Sewing Machine

Machine sewing is such a valuable skill to teach young sewers; it brings ease and efficiency to projects, and it's a tool they can use their whole lives. Sewing with a machine can be intimidating at first, so take your time in showing, teaching, and completing any project. Perhaps the most daunting part of machine sewing is actually setting up the machine, so we'll walk through the steps to get everything set up just right.

## Supplies

As you gather the items in the Basic Machine-Sewing Tool Kit (see next page), you'll see that some of the supplies are also listed in the Hand-Sewing Tool Kit on page 9 (and are described on those pages). Tools are listed separately because most projects use either one kit or the other, but feel free to combine the supplies.

### SEWING MACHINE

Sewing machines vary slightly between brands, but don't worry too much about that; at the root of it they all accomplish the same thing. If you're shopping for a new machine, be sure to visit your local fabric store to learn more about each brand. And even though you're working with kids, it's best not to work with a child's sewing machine or "craft" machine; these are not as well made as real sewing machines, so they tend to be unreliable and more difficult to work with.

Set up your machine on a sturdy surface, such as a desk or table, and find a couple of comfy chairs that allow plenty of room for you to work side-by-side with your young sewer.

## BASIC MACHINE-SEWING TOOL KIT

- Sewing machine
- Sewing-machine needles
- Thread
- Bobbins
- Scissors
- Straight pins
- Pincushion or magnetic pin dish

- Rotary cutter
- Large cutting mat
- Quilter's ruler
- Pinking shears
- Fabric spray adhesive
- Tape measure
- Seam ripper
- Marking tools

## NEEDLES

Your sewing machine will include a selection of needles, but it's good to have a back-up set just in case the original needles should break or grow dull. Refer to your sewing machine manual for the correct type of needles to buy for your machine.

## THREAD

Many of the same thread types available for hand sewing (page 8) are also available for machine sewing. As a quick tip, be sure that the thread you select for machine sewing indicates that it is sewing machine–appropriate.

## BOBBINS

Projects completed using a sewing machine are typically much sturdier than hand-sewn projects, because two threads are involved: an upper thread that comes from the main spool and a lower thread that comes from inside the machine on a bobbin. A bobbin is basically a small spool that you fill with thread yourself. Sewing machines typically come with two or three bobbins, but it's a good idea to have more than that on hand. You can fill them with threads in different colors and avoid having to unwind a bobbin every time you need a new color. To buy more bobbins, take one of the bobbins that originally came with your sewing machine to your local fabric or craft store so you can buy the exact same ones, or refer to the machine's manual for bobbin details.

## CUTTING TOOLS

A rotary cutter, large cutting mat, and quilter's ruler are key for cutting sizeable amounts of fabric quickly and accurately. For best results, use a cutting mat that is 23 inches (58.4 cm) square. This large size will help with precise rotary cutting on most fabrics. Use all three of these tools in conjunction with each other by laying the large cutting mat down on a sturdy surface, placing the fabric flat on the mat, and then using the quilter's ruler to create a straight edge for your rotary cutter.

In addition to sewing scissors (see Scissors, page 8), have a pair of pinking shears on hand. Pinking shears have a zigzag edge rather than a straight edge, which prevents the edges from fraying. Some sewers choose to serge fabrics rather than pink them, but since you'll be working with kids to complete the projects in this book, pinking the edges to finish them will be quicker and easier.

The projects in this book will include details about fabric measurements, so read closely before you cut. Any necessary project templates are included in the book as well.

## A SAFETY NOTE ABOUT ROTARY CUTTERS

Rotary cutters contain an extremely sharp circular blade. Utmost caution needs to be used when handling these cutters. It is strongly advised that rotary cutting be done by an adult. When the cutter is not in use, the safety lever should always be engaged and put away, out of the reach of children.

### FABRIC SPRAY ADHESIVE

Fabric spray adhesive temporarily bonds fabric pieces so you can stitch them together without worrying about them shifting. It's a great tool to have on hand to stabilize fabrics as you're sewing.

### TAPE MEASURE

A thick, floppy tape measure is a great investment for any sewer. Most items you end up sewing will be longer than a ruler and won't be rigid, so having a tape measure on hand will make the job of taking measurements much easier.

## Sewing Machine Basics

Sewing machines vary slightly between brands and styles, but the basic concepts for setting them up and working with them are similar enough that we can go over it here. Be sure to refer to your machine manual for specifics.

### GETTING TO KNOW YOUR MACHINE

Teaching children the different parts of the machine provides an important foundation for their sewing experience. Before starting any actual sewing, walk them through the different parts of the machine they need to understand. Some advanced machines may have several more parts than basic machines, but here are a few parts that any beginner needs to know before they begin.

- The **needle** moves the thread through the fabric. Unlike a hand-sewing needle, a machine-sewing needle's eye is just above the point.

- The **presser foot** is used to keep your fabric flat and secure as you stitch. Remind your young sewer that the presser foot must always be down, touching the fabric, before you can begin sewing.

- The **feed dogs** are the metal teeth on the needle plate that guide your fabric as you sew.

- The **bobbin cover** protects the bobbin mechanism, and must be removed in order to take out the bobbin to thread it.

- The **bobbin winder** keeps the thread taut as you wind your bobbin.

- The **spool pin** keeps the spool of thread in place while sewing.

- The **thread guides** direct you in threading your machine, and keep the thread in place as you sew.

- The **hand wheel** allows you to manually stitch.

- **Tension control** lets you adjust how loose or tight your stitches are; there are also dials that let you adjust your stitch type and stitch length.

- Finally, the **foot pedal** regulates the speed at which your needle moves up and down through the fabric.

### SETTING UP

Once you've found a sturdy place to set up your sewing machine with your young sewer, place the foot pedal on the ground so you (and/or your young sewer if he or she is old enough to handle the pedal) can reach it comfortably.

The next step in setting up your sewing machine is filling the bobbins and threading the machine. This is an exciting step for young sewers—it seems like magic to watch the thread move through the machine and fill up the tiny bobbin. Be sure to check your machine's manual for specifics on both filling the bobbin and threading your machine, and help explain the process to your child as you prepare the machine for sewing.

# A MACHINE-SEWING CHECKLIST

Though each project in this book will vary in steps, here is the basic order of events that you can go through with your child for machine-sewing projects:

1. Prepare your fabric by washing and ironing it per the manufacturer's instructions.

2. Thread your machine, then choose the stitch length and stitch type using the machine's dials.

3. Manually turn the hand wheel until the needle is in the highest position.

4. Make sure the top thread and bobbin thread are pulled together out of the back of the machine, with about 6 inches (15.2 cm) to spare.

5. Place the fabric under the needle, paying close attention to seam allowance.

6. Bring down the presser foot.

7. Put your fingers on the fabric to guide it, being careful to place your fingers far enough away from the needle so there's no risk of your fingers getting caught.

8. Press down gently on the foot pedal and begin sewing.

9. Once you've reached the end, stop the needle in its uppermost position. Lift the presser foot, gently pull out the fabric, and cut the threads, leaving about 6 inches (15.2 cm) of thread still in the machine.

## Sewing Machine Stitches

A sewing machine can produce countless types of stitches, particularly if you have an advanced model. For kid-friendly projects, however, we really only need to worry about a few types.

- A **straight stitch** is the most common stitch we'll use in this book; true to its name, this stitch is straight and most similar to a running hand-stitch.

- A **zigzag stitch** is another straightforward stitch; it's used to give a little more stretch to fabric, particularly around curves and on projects that require both strength and movement. It's also useful for finishing off seams in a practical and fun way.

- A **backstitch** is when you sew backward and forward at the beginning and end of a seam to secure it. Refer to your instruction manual to learn how to stitch in reverse.

# Machine Sewing
# With Kids

Just as with hand sewing, it's best to take it slow when teaching kids to machine sew—perhaps even more so because a sewing machine can be dangerous if used improperly. Take into consideration skill and age when machine sewing with kids, and remember that there's no rush to teach everything in one day. Perhaps you start by holding the pins and controlling the foot pedal while the child focuses solely on moving the fabric, or maybe you start by having the machine all threaded and ready to go.

Practicing on scrap fabric is another good place to begin. Help your young sewers figure out how to sit comfortably so that they can hold the fabric securely and reach the foot pedal. Show them where to place their hands so their fingers are well beyond the reach of the needle and not in the way of the thread. For a particularly young or inexperienced sewer, it may be a good idea for you to handle the foot pedal while the child handles the fabric, until he or she can progress to handling everything at once. You could also start by placing your hands on top of your young sewer's hands, so he or she knows right where the hands should go.

Here are a few methods for helping your child become more comfortable with the sewing machine:

- Draw a line on a scrap of fabric with a water-soluble marker, and have the child sew on the line to practice stitches. Choose thread that contrasts the fabric color so the child can see the stitches clearly.

- Have your young sewer practice feeding the fabric through the presser foot slowly. You could even try this before threading the machine, so your young sewer can focus on feeling how the presser foot keeps the fabric tight and the feed dogs pull it along.

- Teach your young sewer how to press down on the foot pedal gently to adjust the speed. If he or she is having trouble controlling the speed, place a kitchen sponge underneath the pedal to slow it down.

- Show the child the different dials that control stitch type and stitch length, and have them practice changing those dials, stitching a few inches, and then changing the dials again. This will help them see the different stitches available and help them understand stitch length.

- Have your young sewer practice stitching in reverse while explaining to them the importance of backstitching to strengthen seams.

- One tricky part of machine sewing is working with pins. Show your child first how to pin fabrics together, with all the pin heads pointing the same direction. Then show them how to pull out pins and place them directly into a pincushion or magnetic pin dish while sewing at a consistent speed. Practicing this, even without thread, will be very useful in learning pin safety.

- Help your child understand seam allowance by placing a length of painter's tape 1 inch (2.5 cm) away from the edge, then 2 inches (5.1 cm) away, and so forth. Then help them understand that in general, the presser foot gives them a set seam allowance to always follow.

## SEWING SAFETY TIPS

One of the most important things you can teach young sewers is to practice safe sewing. Here are some tips that will ensure they are sewing safely:

- Always work with age-appropriate supplies, and keep any potentially harmful supplies out of reach when not in use.

- Establish rules from the beginning, including that sewing can only be done with adult supervision.

- Never put pins in your mouth; place them directly into a pincushion or magnetic pin dish so they don't fall on the floor and hurt someone.

- Never put your fingers on the presser foot; beginners have no reason to put their fingers anywhere near it.

As a teacher, take into consideration skill and age when machine sewing with kids, and remember that patience and praise go a long way. There are many different ways you can work with a young sewer that will allow them to learn at a pace you are both comfortable with.

# Machine Sewing Troubleshooting

If your machine's having any problems, there are some things you can try before taking it into a repair shop.

- First, if your thread seems to be jammed or your machine is making weird noises, pull the spool of thread off the spool pin and re-thread your machine. The thread could have come off one of the thread guides, or the bobbin could be caught on something. If re-threading the machine doesn't do it, you could also re-wind the bobbin.

- If your bobbin runs out of thread mid-project, lift up the presser foot, take out the fabric, cut the thread, and re-wind the bobbin. Then re-sew about 1 inch (2.5 cm) from where you left off to secure the thread again.

- Another common problem is the thread coming out of the needle. This can be caused by the needle being on backward, so check to make sure the needle is on properly. Also check to make sure the point of the needle hasn't broken off, and replace the needle if necessary.

- If you've tried a few things and your machine still seems off, take it to a repair shop to have a professional look at it. Sewing machines are delicate, so it's better to be safe than sorry.

# Embroidery and Appliqué

Embroidery is the art of adding beautiful stitches that are meant to be seen, as compared to sewing stitches that are generally meant to be hidden. Embroidery stitches are usually displayed in fun colors and unique shapes. Appliqué, another fun embellishment, allows you to sew fabric pieces and shapes to a larger background fabric. Usually hand-sewn, this free-style layering of fabric and textures can add a whole new element to a project.

## Supplies and Techniques

In addition to the selection of hand-sewing needles in your tool kit (page 9), projects that include embroidery will require a hoop and floss specific to the project. These will be noted in the project's "Gather" list as needed, along with any image transfer materials.

Embroidery stitches vary slightly from hand stitches. At right are the primary stitches you need to know.

**backstitch**

**satin stitch**

**straight stitch**

**French knot**

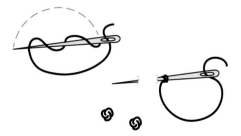

# Transferring Images and Motifs

Some of the projects in this book involve transferring an image or motif onto fabric before sewing. The projects will tell you if this step is necessary, and any motifs will be provided in the back of the book. There are many ways you can transfer a motif or image to fabric, and it comes down to fabric selection and personal preference. Play around with the different methods until you find what works for you and your specific project. Here are three common ways to transfer:

- To use the **tracing method**, trace the image onto the fabric using a water-soluble marker and a good source of light. To remove the marks later, pat the fabric with a damp cloth.

- For the **iron-on method**, make a reverse laser photocopy of the image. Lay the fabric down on an ironing board, place the photocopy facedown on the fabric, and then iron directly over the photocopy. The image will be permanent with this method, so keep that in mind when choosing.

- For the **tissue paper method**, trace your motif onto thin tissue paper, then pin the tissue paper to your fabric. Stitch through the paper and fabric, and then once you're finished, you can rip the tissue paper away from the fabric. Use a needle or tweezers to catch the little edges of paper that may be stuck underneath the stitches.

Once the stitching of the image is complete, it's time to remove any transfer lines. If you used a nonpermanent fabric marker or tailor's chalk to trace the motif, gently rinse it out with water. You may need to rub a small amount of a gentle detergent between your fingers, but the marker should come out without any problems. Lay the fabric flat to dry.

# Appliqué Basics

Appliqué projects often involve templates, which are provided in this book. Simply follow project instructions for cutting and sewing them onto fabric, using either small sewing stitches or fun embroidery stitches.

One of the easiest ways to work with appliqué is to use paper-lined fusible web, as follows:

**1** Enlarge and cut out the template shape per the project instructions.

**2** Turn the template over to reverse it, then trace it onto the paper side of the fusible web.

**3** Cut out the shape, leaving an allowance on all sides of at least ¼ inch (6 mm).

**4** Following the manufacturer's directions, fuse the non-paper side of the web onto the wrong side of the fabric.

**5** Cut out the template on the marked lines.

**6** Remove the paper from the fusible web, and fuse the cut-out to the background fabrics.

## Stuffing Basics

Some of the projects in this book use stuffing to create three-dimensional objects such as pillows and dolls. Stuffing is commonly available in 100 percent polyester, but each brand and type has a different feel. Explore different kinds until you find one that you like and that fits the project at hand. In addition, a good stuffing tool is useful. You can find different kinds in craft stores, but the cheap and simple solution is to use the end of a wooden spoon, an

unsharpened pencil, or a chopstick—anything that's going to help you get stuffing into tight crevices.

Once the doll or pillow is stitched and turned right-side-out, start by pulling a generous handful of stuffing loose from its packaging, and fluff it a bit to remove any lumps. Then begin to work the stuffing inside the pillow or doll. Start at the edge furthest away from the opening, using your fingers and stuffing tool to push the stuffing into the corners. Keep stuffing until the project is full. Pay careful attention to how you want the final project to look, because once the opening is sewn shut, it's hard to change how the stuffing sits. Once you are satisfied, hand sew the opening closed.

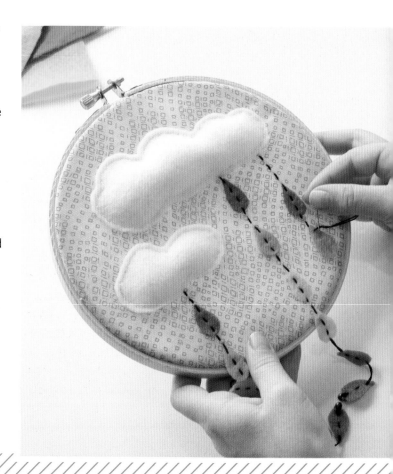

## FOR THE LOVE OF FELT

Many projects in this book utilize felt, either as a base or as an embellishment. When you're purchasing felt for your projects, keep in mind that felt can be bought two ways: by the sheet, which usually measures 9 x 12 inches (22.9 x 30.5 cm), or by the yard.

To determine which type of felt you need to buy, simply take a close look at the measurements noted by the felt in the materials list for each project. From there you'll be able to see whether you can cut the amount of felt you need from a 9 x 12-inch (22.9 x 30.5 cm) sheet, or whether you might need to buy it by the yard.

## A Family Affair

There is such joy in sharing the age-old tradition of sewing with young sewers, and that joy is tenfold when you have multiple young sewers to teach. If you're working with more than one small child, consider giving them different tasks so everyone is involved and part of the process. If they're different ages, split up tasks based on ability—for example, a younger child could pick out fabric colors and help you cut out patterns while an older child could do more of the sewing. One child can trace images while another works on hand sewing, or one child can stuff a pillow while another practices embroidery stitches—the possibilities are endless for ways to split up the projects. The more involved everyone is, the more they will feel ownership of the final result and the more exciting it will be.

# FOX FRIEND

**Designer:** AIMEE RAY

This cute, plush fox doll is easy to sew and fun to customize with a few embroidery stitches.

## Gather

- Basic Hand-Sewing Tool Kit (page 9)
- Fox Friend templates (page 110)
- Flower motif and stitch guide (page 26)
- Three sheets of 9 x 12-inch (22.9 x 30.5 cm) craft felt: orange, white, and dark brown
- Tissue paper
- Embroidery floss, 1 skein each of green, orange, dark orange, dark brown and white*
- Tweezers
- Polyester fiberfill, 1 ounce

*The designer used DMC embroidery floss 166, 352, 351, 2371, and 316*

**Finished Dimensions:**
5 inches (12.7 cm) tall

## Make

**1** Trace the templates onto the craft felt as follows. Use white tailor's chalk to trace onto orange and brown, and a pencil to trace onto white. Then cut out the pieces.

- Template A (front and back): cut 2 from orange felt
- Template B (face and belly): cut 1 from white felt
- Template C (tail accent): cut 1 from white felt
- Template D (ear accent): cut 2 from white felt
- Template E (eyes): cut 2 eyes from dark brown felt
- Template F (nose): cut 1 from dark brown felt

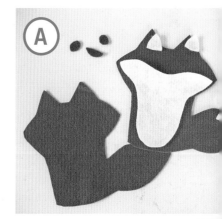

**2** Pin the white ears and face/belly pieces onto one of the orange cut pieces, referring to photo Ⓐ for placement. With a hand-embroidery needle and white embroidery floss, stitch them in place using the stab stitch, which is a variation of the straight stitch made with much tinier stitch lengths Ⓑ.

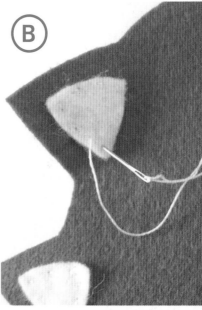

**3** Pin the white tail accent onto the orange tail, aligning the points. Use the stab stitch to sew along the wavy edge, but not around the point. Then turn the piece over to the backside and trim off the point of the orange felt. This will allow you to sew the front and back of the fox together without the added thickness at the tail area Ⓒ.

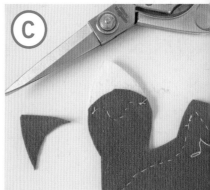

**4** Pin the eyes and nose to the face. With a hand-embroidery needle and dark brown embroidery floss, stitch them in place using the stab stitch. Use white floss to stitch accents on each eye Ⓓ.

**5** Use a pencil to trace the flower motif onto a piece of tissue paper. Pin the tissue paper onto the belly portion of the fox. Use the flower motif stitch guide to embroider the motif through both thicknesses of felt. Carefully tear away the tissue paper and discard. Use tweezers to pull away any small pieces of tissue paper.

**6** Pin the front and back pieces of the fox together, wrong sides facing. With dark orange thread and starting at the bottom of the body, use a whipstitch to sew the pieces together Ⓔ. For the white tail portion, change to white thread and continue stitching, then switch back to dark orange. When you have about 2 inches (5.1 cm) left to sew shut, stuff the fox with polyester fiberfill until it is nice and tight, then complete the stitching Ⓕ.

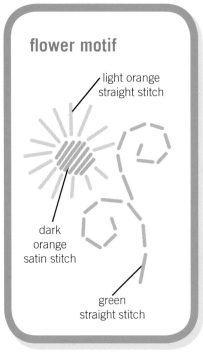

**flower motif**

light orange straight stitch

dark orange satin stitch

green straight stitch

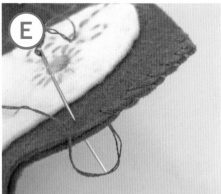

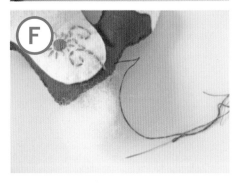

## aimee's Tips

- Create your own embroidery designs by drawing any flower or shape you like.

- Try using different colors of felt. For example, use grays to make a wolf doll.

# KITTY CAT PILLOW

**Designer:** ANNABEL WRIGLEY

Adjust the size of the templates to make this pillow whatever size you like.

## Gather

- Basic Machine-Sewing Tool Kit (page 13)
- Kitty Cat Pillow templates (page 117)
- 2 pieces of natural cotton twill fabric, 13 inches (33 cm) square
- 1 piece of wool felt, 12 x 10 inches (30.5 x 25.4 cm)
- 6-strand embroidery floss: one skein each of black and coral
- Polyester fiberfill, 10 ounces
- Stuffing tool

**Finished Dimensions:**

14 inches (35.6 cm) square

**Seam allowance:**

¼ inch (6 mm)

## Make

**1** Enlarge and use templates to cut the following pieces:
  - Template A (front and back): Cut 2 from cotton twill fabric and mark the "no sew" section at the top of the head.
  - Template B (face): Cut 1 from the wool felt

**2** Center and pin the felt piece from Template B onto the right side of one of the cotton pieces from Template A Ⓐ. The placement of the felt is not specific, so pin it where you like; just be sure to leave enough room for the seam allowance. Stitch the felt onto the cotton, around the edge of the entire felt piece Ⓑ.

**3** Use a water-soluble marker to draw simple eyes, nose, and mouth onto the felt. If you are not happy with any of the markings, dab it with a damp cloth and they will quickly disappear. Then redraw the face until you are happy with the way things look.

**4** Use black embroidery floss to make a small cluster of long straight stitches for the eyes. Use coral embroidery floss to make a small cluster of satin stitches for the nose. Use black embroidery floss to make a few backstitches for the mouth and the line that connects the mouth to the nose Ⓒ.

**5** Pin the two cotton pieces with right sides together. Starting at the top of the head, sew along the entire edge of the layers, making sure to avoid the "no sew" section at the top.

**6** Clip the curved seams at approximately every 1 inch (2.5 cm) Ⓓ.

**7** Turn the pillow right side out and stuff it with polyester fiberfill until it reaches a firmness that you like. Use a stuffing tool to push stuffing into all of the corners.

**8** Pin the opening closed and sew with a whipstitch.

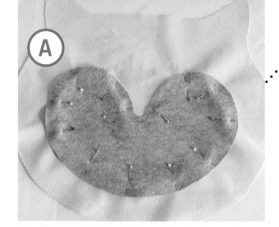

A

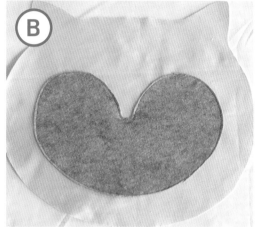

B

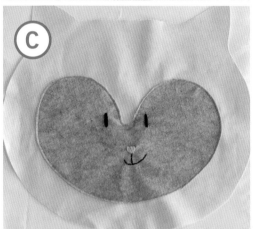

C

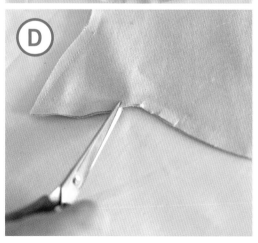

D

## annabel's Tips

- Invite your child to draw the face of the cat. This will make the pillow uniquely his or hers.

- Use different types of fabrics and felts to create different looks.

# CLOUDS AND RAINDROPS HOOP ART

**Designer:** CYNTHIA SHAFFER

Here's a great project for a rainy day—a hoop of puffy clouds, and raindrops made with all colors of the rainbow.

# Gather

- Basic Hand-Sewing Tool Kit (page 9)
- Cloud and raindrop templates (page 115)
- 1 piece of quilter's cotton in turquoise blue, 8 inches (20.3 cm) square
- 1 piece of thin batting, 8 inches (20.3 cm) square
- Wooden embroidery hoop, 6 inches (15.2 cm) diameter
- 1 piece of white craft felt, 6 x 4 inches (15.2 x 10.2 cm)
- Scraps of craft felt in red, orange, yellow, lime green, turquoise, and purple

- Tiny amount of polyester fiberfill and a stuffing tool
- Glue stick
- Perle cotton (size 5), 1 skein of black
- 3 small black beads with holes large enough to go through a hand-sewing needle
- ½ inch (1.3 cm) ribbon, 18 inches (45.7 cm) long

**Finished Dimensions:**

The hoop plus the dangling raindrops measures 6 x 10½ inches (15.2 x 26.7 cm)

# Make

**1** Place the turquoise fabric on the work surface with the wrong side facing you. Place the batting on top of the fabric.

**2** Center the inner ring of the embroidery hoop on the batting and then flip everything over. Push the outer ring of the embroidery hoop onto the inner hoop. Adjust the screw to accommodate the fabric and batting.

**3** Use Templates A, B, and C to trace and cut the following:
- Template A (large cloud): cut 1 from white felt
- Template B (small cloud): cut 1 from white felt
- Template C (rain drop): cut 3 each from red, orange, yellow, lime green, turquoise, and purple felt for a total of 18 raindrops.

**4** Pin both clouds to the hooped fabric, positioning them as seen in the photo on page 30, with the hoop's connecting screw centered at the top. One at a time, stitch the felt onto the fabric with a running stitch, using white thread and a hand-sewing needle, stopping when you are about 2 inches (5.1 cm) from the spot where you started stitching Ⓐ.

**5** For each cloud, remove the pin and insert a small amount of fiberfill into the opening. Use a stuffing tool to push the fiberfill into the edges of the cloud Ⓑ. Stitch the opening closed.

**6** Use a small amount of glue from a glue stick to position and lightly adhere the red and orange raindrops and one of the yellow raindrops onto the turquoise fabric.

**7** To sew each column of raindrops, start a running stitch with black perle cotton at the bottom of a cloud, then sew a straight line down the turquoise background and through each raindrop, making a few stitches between them. When you reach the edge of the hoop, stitch through the remaining raindrops in order as shown, leaving a stretch of thread between them Ⓒ.

**8** Knot the perle cotton when you reach the end of each purple raindrop. Slide a black bead onto the needle and push it up to the end of the purple raindrop and then stitch it onto the end. Knot the perle cotton and cut the thread close to the knot Ⓓ.

**9** Flip the hoop over to the backside and cut off the excess fabric close to the hoop. Flip the hoop back to the front and push the outer embroidery hoop back a bit to make the background fabric stand out, being careful to not push it off completely.

**10** Loop the ribbon through the top of the hoop at the screw, and tie the ends together for hanging.

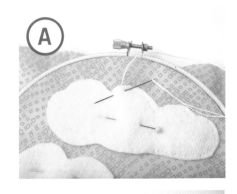

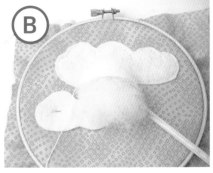

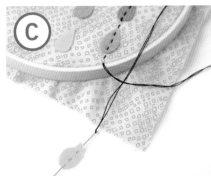

## cynthia's Tips

Try sketching different motifs! Here are some ideas:

- Boat with fishing pole and dangling fish
- Spider web with a dangling spider
- Umbrella with dangling raindrops

# WOODLAND PUPPETS

**Designer:** CYNTHIA SHAFFER

All three of these puppets share the same body template. The different felt colors and shapes, plus the eyes, ears, and chest details, make each unique personality come to life.

# Gather

## For All Puppets

- Basic Machine-Sewing Tool Kit (page 13)
- Puppet Templates (pages 111–114)
- Perle cotton (size 5), 1 skein of black
- White craft glue
- Black thread

## Hedgehog

- 4 pieces of 9 x 12 inches (2.9 x 30.5 cm) craft felt: light brown, brown, black, and cream
- 1 black button, ½ inch (1.3 cm) diameter

## Squirrel

- 1 piece of light gray felt, 9 x 12 inches (22.9 x 30.5 cm)
- 1 piece of dark gray felt, 4 x 7 inches (10.2 x 17.8 cm)
- 1 piece of white felt, 5 x 6½ inches (12.7 x 16.5 cm)
- Scrap of hot pink felt

## Owl

- 1 piece of brown felt, 9 x 12 inches (22.9 x 30.5 cm)
- 1 piece of cream felt, 4 x 6 inches (10.2 x 15.2 cm)
- 1 piece of white felt, 4 x 3½ inches (10.2 x 8.9 cm)
- 1 piece of yellow felt, 3½ x 2½ inches (8.9 x 6.4 cm)
- Scrap of black felt
- 1 piece of tan felt, 6 x 5 inches (15.2 x 12.7 cm)
- 2 black buttons, ½ inch (1.3 cm) diameter

## Finished Dimensions:

All puppets are 6½ inches (16.5 cm) wide by 8½ to 9 inches (21.6 to 22.9 cm) tall

## Seam Allowance:

⅛ inch (3 mm)

# Make

## THE HEDGEHOG

**1** Use templates to trace and cut the following, making sure to transfer all placement markings from the templates to the cut felt pieces:
- Template A (body): Cut 2 from the light brown felt
- Template B (arms): Cut 2 from the brown felt
- Template H (face): Cut 1 from the brown felt
- Template C (ears): Cut 2 from the cream felt
- Template G (chest): Cut 1 from the cream felt

**2** Pin the cream chest piece on one of the body pieces. Layer the face on top of the chest piece and pin. Tuck the ears under the face at the ear placement marks and pin.

**3** With black thread, machine-stitch around the face, catching the ears. Then stitch around the chest piece.

**4** Make large and random long stitches on the light brown felt with the perle cotton, radiating out from the chest piece Ⓐ.

**5** Stitch the button nose in place. Pin the arms to the puppet body at the arm placement marks Ⓑ.

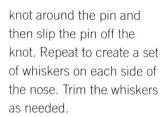

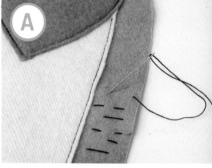

**6** Make French knots for the eyes.

**7** To make the whiskers, knot 2 strands of black perle cotton and stitch from the back to the front. Form a knot on the front and then poke a pin through the loop of the knot before pulling the knot tight. Tighten the

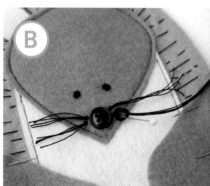

knot around the pin and then slip the pin off the knot. Repeat to create a set of whiskers on each side of the nose. Trim the whiskers as needed.

**8** Pin the back of the puppet to the front and stitch around the outer perimeter, backstitching at the beginning and at the end. Do not stitch across the bottom, and take care not to stitch down the ears ⓒ.

**9** Cut a strip of black felt that measures 1¼ x 19 inches (3.2 x 48.3 cm). Use pinking shears to cut one of the edges.

**10** Snip into the strip starting at the pinked edge and stopping ¼ inch (6 mm) from the edge. Make snips along the entire strip ¼ inch (6 mm) apart.

**11** Flip the puppet so that the backside is up. Mark ½ inch (1.3 cm) in from the outer edge with a pencil. Apply a thin line of white glue along the marks. Carefully lay the black felt strip into the glue at the marks, curving the strip as it reaches the curved top portion of the puppet. Let dry ⓓ.

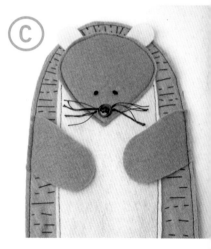

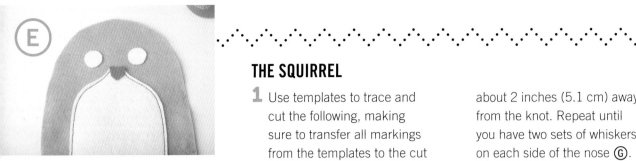

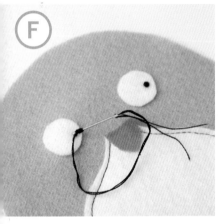

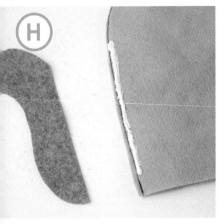

## THE SQUIRREL

**1** Use templates to trace and cut the following, making sure to transfer all markings from the templates to the cut felt pieces:

- Template A (body): Cut 2 from the light gray felt
- Template B (arms): Cut 2 from the light gray felt
- Template C (ears): Cut 2 from the dark gray felt
- Template D (chest): Cut 1 from the white felt
- Template E (tail): Cut 1 from the dark gray felt
- Template F (nose): Cut 1 from the hot pink felt scrap

**2** Use a dime and trace and cut out two pieces for the eyes from the white felt.

**3** Center and pin the white chest piece on one of the light gray body pieces. Stitch around the perimeter of the white chest piece with black thread.

**4** Glue the nose and the eyes in place and let dry **E**.

**5** Use the perle cotton to make French knots for the eyes and small back stitches to make the mouth **F**.

**6** To make the whiskers, take a small stitch near the nose with perle cotton, knot, then clip

about 2 inches (5.1 cm) away from the knot. Repeat until you have two sets of whiskers on each side of the nose **G**.

**7** Pin the ears to the puppet body at the marks then pin the back of the puppet to the front and stitch around the perimeter. Do not stitch across the bottom.

**8** Apply a line of white glue to the back left side of the puppet, ½ inch (1.3 cm) from the bottom and continuing for 5 inches (12.7 cm). Press the tail into the glue and set aside to dry **H**.

## THE OWL

**1** Use templates to trace and cut the following, making sure to transfer all markings from the templates to the cut felt pieces:

- Template A (body): Cut 2 from the brown felt
- Template M (chest): Cut 1 from the cream felt
- Template I (face): Cut 1 from the white felt
- Template J (eyes): Cut 2 from the yellow felt
- Template N (wings): Cut 2 from the tan felt
- Template K (ears): Cut 2 from the brown felt
- Template L (beak): Cut 1 from the black felt

**2** Center and pin the chest and face pieces onto one of the body pieces. Stitch around the perimeter using black thread (I).

**3** Pin the yellow eyes to the owl face, overlapping slightly. Stitch around the eyes using black thread.

**4** Use the perle cotton and stitch the buttons onto the owl eyes. Stitch little "V" shapes onto the cream chest. Backstitch the beak in place at the top edge of the chest (J).

**5** Pin the ears to the wrong side of the front puppet body. Pin the left wing to the wrong side of the front puppet body facing out. Pin the right wing to the right side of the front of the puppet body, facing in.

**6** Pin the back of the puppet body to the front and stitch around the perimeter. Do not stitch across the bottom.

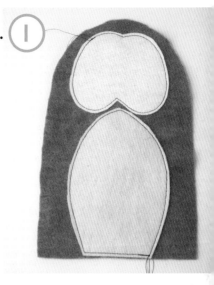

*cynthia's* **Tips**

- Make boy and girl versions of these puppets by slightly changing the color of the bodies.
- Add embellishments such as a felt bow or a felt tie.

# TASSEL AND CIRCLE EARRINGS

**Designer:** ANNABEL WRIGLEY

Earrings stitched with neon thread and colorful felts and fabrics. What's not to love?

# Gather

## For both earrings

- Basic Machine-Sewing Tool Kit (page 13)
- Neon thread for sewing machine
- 1 pair of earring hooks for each pair of earrings
- Needle-nose pliers

## Tassel Earrings

- 2 pieces of felt in bright colors, 2-inch (5.1 cm) square each

- Damp cloth
- Hot glue gun and glue stick
- 2 pieces of neon twine, 1½ inches (3.8 cm) long each

## Circle Earrings

- Adhesive interfacing, 5 inches (12.7 cm) square
- Spool of thread (or other item that can be used as a circle template)
- Fabric scraps
- 2 pieces of neon twine, 2¼ inches (5.7 cm) long each

## Finished Dimensions:

Tassel Earrings are ½ x 2 inches (1.3 x 5.1 cm); Circle Earrings are 1½ inches (3.8 cm) diameter

# Make

## TASSEL EARRINGS

**1** On one of the felt pieces, use a water-soluble marker and ruler to make a straight line, ½ inch (1.3 cm) from one of the edges.

**2** Thread your sewing machine with neon thread and sew zigzag and straight stitches within that ½-inch (1.3 cm) space. Then dab the felt with a damp cloth to remove the line.

**3** Use scissors to snip the felt, starting from the edge opposite the stitch line. Continue making snips approximately every ⅛ inch (3 mm) Ⓐ.

**4** Apply a small dab of hot glue on the top end of the fringe. Fold the neon twine in half and stick the ends into the hot glue, making sure there is a little twine loop sticking up from the top of the fringe Ⓑ.

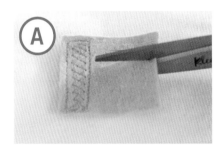

**5** Run a line of hot glue along the top of the fringe and tightly roll it into a tassel before the glue dries, making sure to start rolling from the end with the twine.

**6** Use needle-nose pliers to attach the earing hook to the neon twine. Repeat these steps for the second earring.

## CIRCLE EARRINGS

**1** Lay the adhesive interfacing flat on a work surface. With the circle template and a pencil, trace four circles and cut out. Both sides of the interfacing will have paper backing so it doesn't matter which side you trace.

**2** For each circle, peel off the paper backing on one side and press the sticky side onto the wrong side of a fabric scrap. If you are using a patterned fabric, be mindful of where you place the circle so that the part of the pattern you like will be on the earring. Cut around the fabric so that it is the same size as the circle Ⓒ Ⓓ.

**3** For two of the circles, peel the backing paper from the remaining side. Fold one of the neon twine pieces in half and place it on this sticky side,

making sure that the folded loop peeks above the top of the circle Ⓔ.

**4** Remove the backing paper from the remaining circles and press each one against a twined circle, sandwiching the twine between the circles.

**5** Thread your sewing machine with neon thread and stitch along the entire perimeter of the circle. Use a straight stitch or other decorative stitches that your machine allows.

**6** Use needle-nose pliers to attach an earring hook to each neon twine.

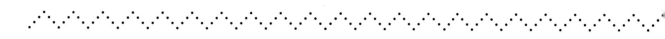

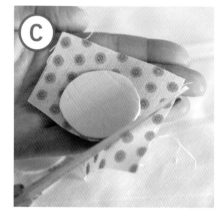
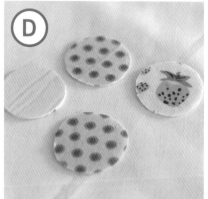
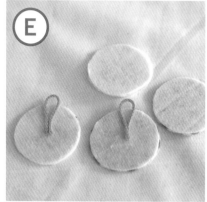

## annabel's Tips

- Try making the tassel earrings with different fabrics or even leather!

- Cut the felt fringe on the tassel earrings narrower or wider, depending on your preferred look.

- Experiment with different decorative stitches on your sewing machine.

# ADJUSTABLE HEADBAND

**Designer:** JENNY DOH

The elastic ponytail holder used to pull this headband together will allow it to fit most children. If you'd like the tied ends to look longer and floppier, or if you'd like to make it for an adult with a larger head, add an inch or two to the length of the fabric pieces you cut.

## Gather

- Basic Machine-Sewing Tool Kit (page 13)
- ¼ yard (.2 m) green patterned quilting cotton fabric
- 1 small elastic ponytail holder

**Finished Dimensions:**

1½ x 33 inches (3.8 x 83.8 cm), untied

**Seam Allowance:**

¼ inch (6 mm)

## Make

1 Use a rotary cutter, quilter's ruler, and cutting mat to cut two fabric pieces that each measure 4 x 16½ inches (10.2 x 41.9 cm).

2 Fold one of the cut fabric pieces in half with right sides facing and the long sides aligned. Press. Repeat with the remaining fabric piece.

3 To make the diagonal bow ends:
- Lay the pressed fabric strip horizontally on a work surface with the folded edge along the bottom.
- Fold over both layers of one of the short ends, until the side edge meets the bottom folded edge to form a triangle. Press and cut through both thicknesses along the diagonal fold.
- Machine-stitch along the diagonal and the long open side, through both thicknesses. Leave the remaining short side unsewn.
- Trim the fabric at the corners and turn it right side out. Use a pin to pull the corners out Ⓐ Ⓑ (see next page).
- Repeat with the second pressed fabric strip.

**4** Take one of the strips, thread the unsewn end through the ponytail holder, and turn under the end by ¼ inch (6 mm) to enclose the holder. Turn it under another ¼ inch (6 mm) and pin Ⓒ. Hand-sew in place, making sure to go through only one thickness of the main body part of the headband Ⓓ.

**5** Repeat step 4 to attach the remaining fabric strip to the other side of the ponytail holder.

**6** Place the elastic portion of the headband at the back of the wearer's neck and then wrap the two sides of the headband up and over the head. Tie the ends twice to make the headband snug, but not too tight.

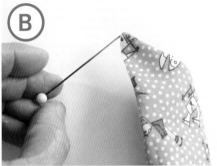

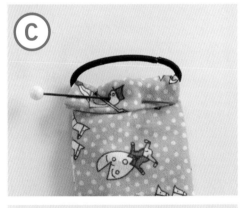

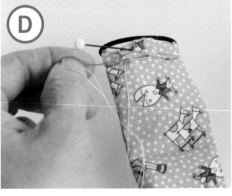

*jenny's*
# Tips

- For a thicker headband, cut the strips wider and use a larger ponytail holder.

- Piece together tiny pieces of fabric from your stash into strips to make a patchwork style headband.

# ALIEN STAND-UP DOLLS

**Designer:** MOLLIE JOHANSON

A small beanbag that gets hidden inside each doll is what allows these aliens to stand up. Make one, or two, or all three with the fun character motifs provided.

# Gather

- Basic Machine-Sewing Tool Kit (page 13)
- Alien templates (page 116)
- Alien motifs and stitch guides (pages 48–49)
- 1 piece of linen or other solid fabric, 9 x 10 inches (22.9 x 25.4 cm), for each doll
- 7-inch (17.8 cm) embroidery hoop
- Perle cotton (size 5) in assorted colors, including black and several variegated
- 1 piece of quilting cotton, 9 x 20 inches (22.9 x 50.8 cm), for each doll
- Rice or dried beans
- Polyester fiberfill, 2 ounces, for each doll

**Finished Dimensions:**

6 x 8 inches (15.2 x 20.3 cm)

**Seam Allowance:**

¼ inch (6 mm)

# Make

**1** Transfer one of the alien motifs onto the linen.

**2** Secure the linen in the embroidery hoop and embroider according to the enlarged stitch guide Ⓐ. Remove any transfer lines as needed.

**3** Enlarge and use the templates to cut the following pieces:
- Template A (front/back): Center the template on top of the embroidered linen. Pin and cut out. Use the same template to cut the back piece from the quilting cotton.
- Template B (base): Cut 3 from the quilting cotton.

**4** With right sides together, machine-stitch the front and back pieces together at one corner and stitch for approximately 1 inch (2.5 cm). Leave a gap of about 3 inches (7.6 cm), then continue stitching around the sides and top, leaving the bottom edge open. Be sure to backstitch each time when you start and stop Ⓑ.

**5** With the doll still wrong side out, pin one of the base pieces into the bottom opening with the right side facing in. Hand-sew it in place with small running stitches Ⓒ.

**6** Notch along the top curve and turn right side out.

**7** With perle cotton and hand-sewing needle, add a top running stitch around the base, close to the seam, to create a flat base Ⓓ.

**8** With wrong sides together, sew the remaining base ovals, leaving a 1-inch (2.5 cm) opening. Fill with rice or beans but do not overfill. Stitch the oval closed to create a small beanbag Ⓔ.

**9** Slip the beanbag into the stand-up doll through the side opening and let it settle into the base Ⓕ. Fill the rest of the doll with fiberfill until it is nice and firm Ⓖ. Hand-sew the opening closed with a slip stitch Ⓗ.

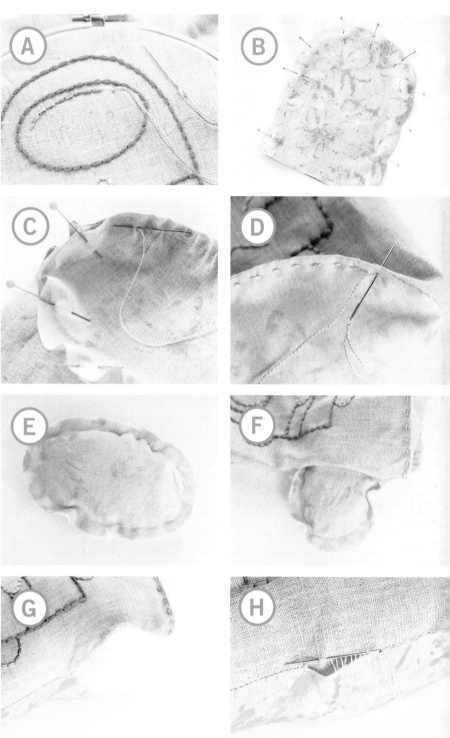

# alien motifs

enlarge 150%

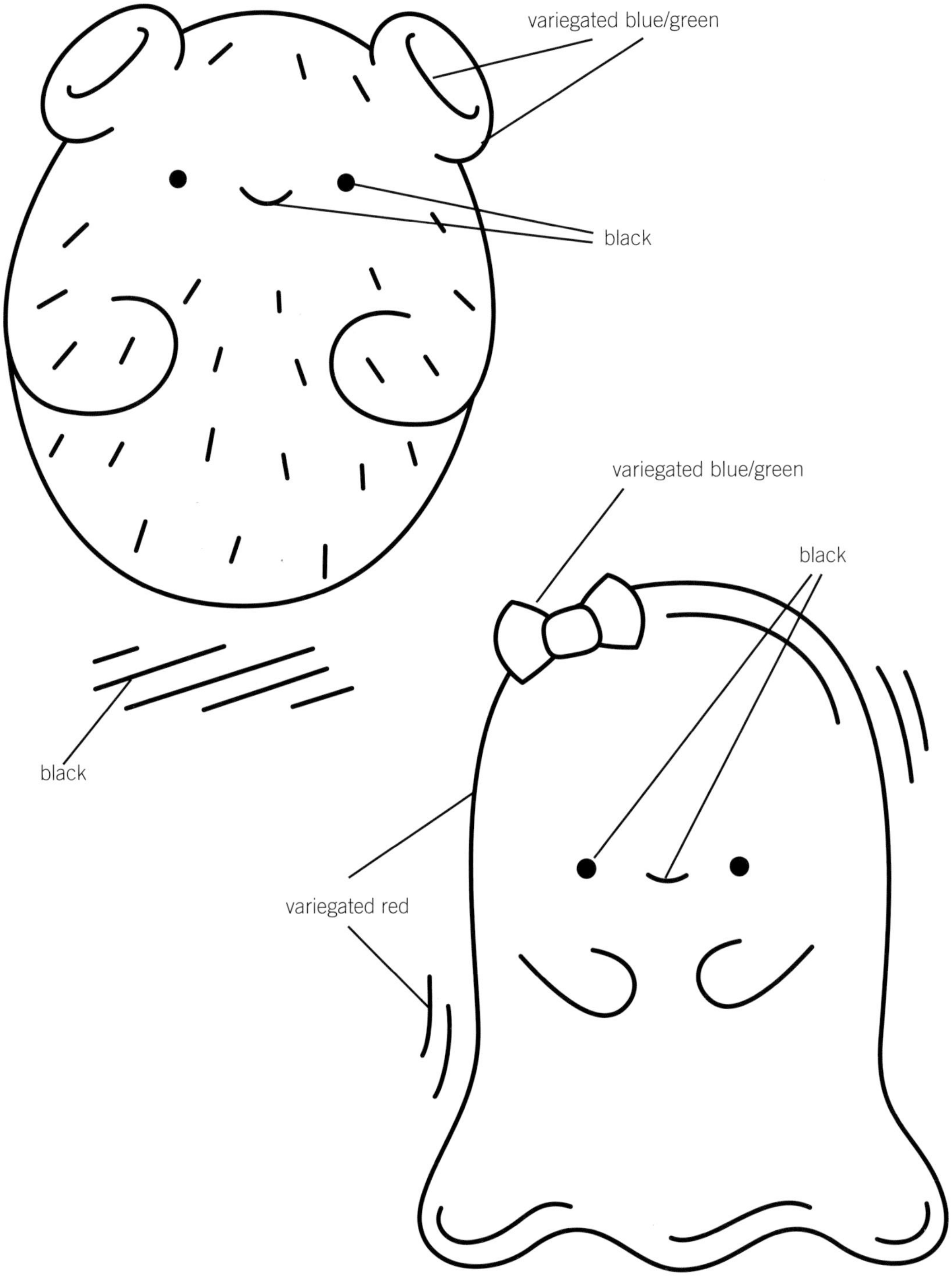

variegated blue/green

black

black

variegated blue/green

black

variegated red

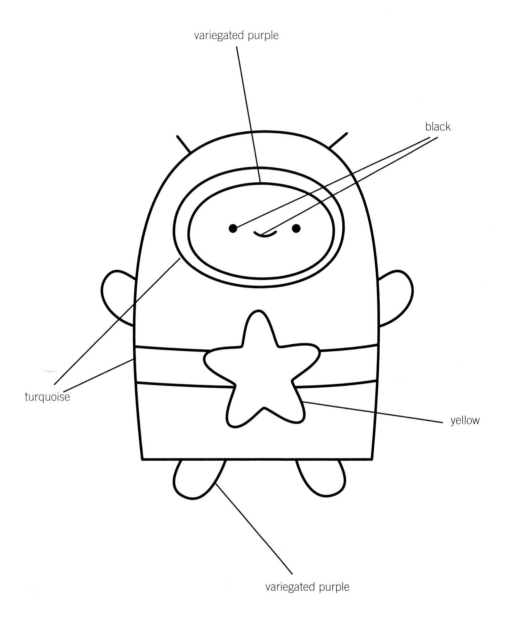

variegated purple

black

turquoise

yellow

variegated purple

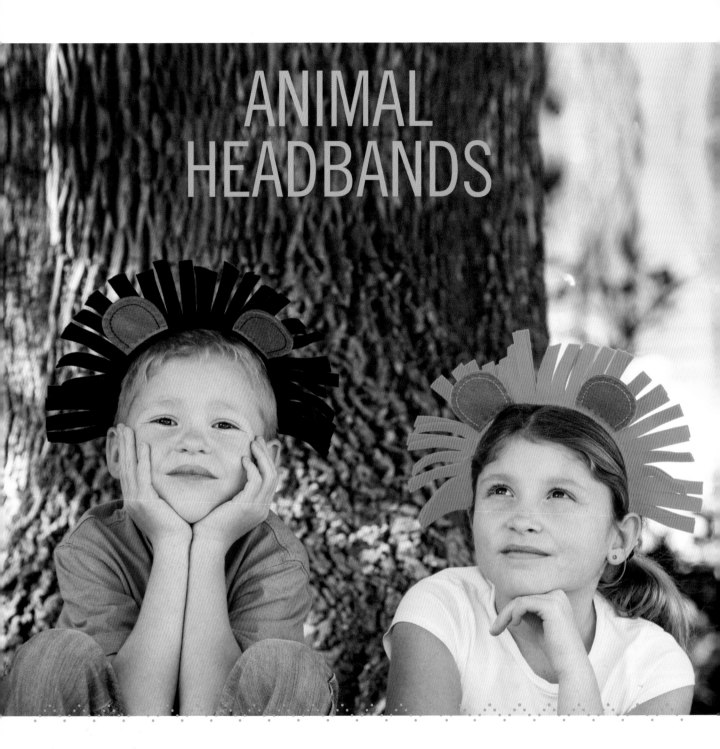

# ANIMAL HEADBANDS

**Designer:** LAURA HOWARD

Unleash your inner lion, deer, or alien with these awesome animal headbands.

# Gather

- Basic Hand-Sewing Tool Kit (page 9)
- Plastic headband with teeth, approximately ⅝ inch (1.6 cm) wide, for each animal headband
- Headband templates (page 120)

### For the Lion

- 1 piece of dark brown or orange felt, 10 x 11 inches (25.4 x 27.9 cm)
- 1 piece of light brown felt, 5 x 6 inches (12.7 x 15.2 cm)
- 1 sheet of plain white paper
- Embroidery floss, 1 skein of dark brown or orange

### For the Deer

- 1 piece of cream felt, 6 x 7 inches (15.2 x 17.8 cm)

- 1 piece of light brown felt, 7 x 8 inches (17.8 x 20.3 cm)
- 1 piece of white felt, 3 x 4 inches (7.6 x 10.2 cm)
- Thread to match each felt color

### For the Alien

- 1 piece of green felt, 9 x 12 inches (22.9 x 30.5 cm)
- 1 piece of white felt, 2 x 5 inches (5.1 x 12.7 cm)
- 1 piece of black felt, 1 x 3 inches (2.5 x 7.6 cm)
- Thread to match each felt color

### Finished Dimensions:

Lion: Mane is 2½ inches (6.35 cm) from headband

Deer: Antlers are 2¾ inches (7 cm) from headband

Alien: Eye stalks are 3¼ inches (8.26 cm) from headband

# Make

### FOR THE LION

**1** Enlarge the templates and cut the following pieces:

- Template A (mane): Cut 3 pieces from dark brown felt, 6 x 4½ inches (15.2 x 11.4)
- Template B (mane cutting guide): Cut 1 from plain white paper
- Template C (ear): Cut 4 from light brown felt
- Template D (ear insert): Cut 2 from light brown felt

**2** Position the cutting guide at the center of one of the dark brown felt pieces and pin. Cut each side of the felt into a fringe, with approximately ½ inch (1.3 cm) between cuts. Stop each cut at the edge of the guide. Repeat this step for the other two dark brown felt pieces Ⓐ (see next page).

**3** Fold one of the mane pieces in half and wrap it around the top center of the headband. As you hold the felt tightly, it should stretch slightly, allowing you to fold around the curve of the headband. With a hand-sewing needle and coordinating thread, sew a line of running stitches through both layers of felt.

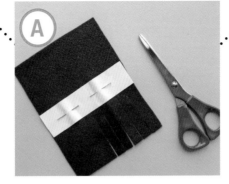

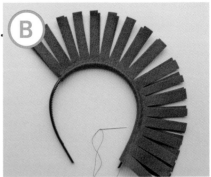

Repeat this step to add the other two pieces on either side of this first piece, flush with each other, to create one continuous fringed mane Ⓑ.

4 With three strands of brown embroidery floss, stitch a curved line on one of the light brown felt ear pieces, using a backstitch. Place this onto a second felt ear piece and place one of the ear inserts in between the two layers. Sew together along the curve slightly above the embroidery with a running stitch, using a coordinating thread. Leave the bottom edge unstitched Ⓒ. Repeat for the second ear.

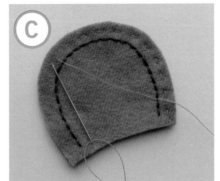

5 Position one of the ears onto the headband so the bottom of the ear is flush with the curve of the headband. Use coordinating thread to sew the ear onto the mane with a line of running stitches along the bottom of the ear through all thicknesses Ⓓ. Repeat to attach the second ear.

## FOR THE DEER

1 Enlarge the templates and cut the following pieces (cut all as mirrored pairs):
   • Template E (antler): Cut 2 from cream felt on a fold
   • Template F (antler insert): Cut 2 from cream felt

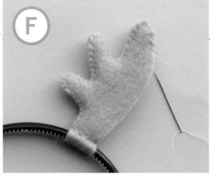

- Template G (ear): Cut 2 from brown felt on a fold
- Template H (ear insert): Cut 2 from brown felt
- Template I (inner ear): Cut 2 from white felt

**2** To make the antlers:
- Fold one of the cream antlers in half and wrap it around the top of the headband so that it is about 1 inch (2.5 cm) from the center of the band. Make sure that the limbs of the antlers are facing the center of the headband.
- Hold the felt tightly around the headband with one hand and sew a line of running stitches close to the headband from side to side to secure Ⓔ.
- Add the antler insert between the front and back of the antler layers and then whipstitch along the entire antler Ⓕ.
- Repeat to make the second antler.

**3** To make the ears:
- Pin a white inner ear to one half of each ear and stitch in place Ⓖ.
- Wrap one ear around the headband, slightly below an

antler, with the straighter edge at the top. Hold the felt tightly around the headband and sew a line of running stitches close to the headband from side to side to secure Ⓗ.
- Add the ear insert between the front and back layers and whipstitch along the entire ear perimeter Ⓘ.
- Repeat to make the second ear.

## FOR THE ALIEN

**1** Enlarge the templates and cut the following pieces:

- Template J (eye stalks): Cut 3 from green felt
- Template K (eye stalk inserts): Cut 3 from green felt
- Template L (white eye): Cut 3 from white felt
- Template M (black pupil): Cut 3 from black felt

**2** Center one of the white eye pieces on one end of a green stalk, then stitch along the perimeter with a running stitch in coordinating thread.

Center a black pupil on the white piece and stitch with coordinating thread Ⓙ. Repeat with remaining pieces.

**3** With wrong sides together, fold a green eye stalk and wrap it around the top center of the headband. Hold the felt tightly around the headband with one hand and sew a line of running stitches close to the headband from side to side to secure Ⓚ. Add the eye stalk insert between the stalk layers and secure with a running stitch along all outer edges Ⓛ.

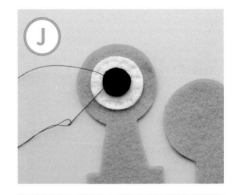

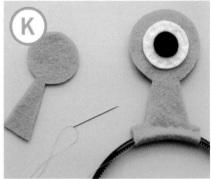

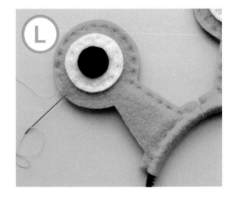

**4** Repeat step 3, with the other eye stalks and attach them to the left and right side of the first eye stalk. Make sure that the stalks are flush with each other.

**Designer:** CHERI HEATON

Use the templates provided or make shapes of your own, then fill these paper pouches with sweets for occasions big and small.

# Gather

- Basic Machine-Sewing Tool Kit (page 13)
- Candy Paper Pouch templates (page 116)
- Papers and paper scraps in assorted patterns and colors, including plain white
- Small piece of colored masking tape
- 2 craft Googly eyes
- Craft glue
- Black permanent marker
- Approximately ¼ cup (2 ounces) of candy to fill each pouch

**Finished Dimensions:**

All pouches are roughly 5 x 6 inches (12.7 x 15.2 cm)

# Make

**1** Cut 2 of each enlarged template from patterned paper, with the ghost cut from white paper.

**2** For each pouch, put wrong sides of the cut papers together and stitch along all edges, leaving an opening large enough to insert candy Ⓐ Ⓑ. Consider the following options as you stitch, stuff, and stitch.

- **Star:** Use a straight stitch, and leave one of the V sections open for inserting the candy.
- **Heart:** Use a zigzag stitch and embellish the front by writing "hello!" on a piece of red masking tape and adhering that to the front of the pouch.
- **Circle:** Before stitching the two sides together, embellish with a mini garland: Cut small triangles in a contrasting piece of paper, and then cut a slightly curved strip of white paper. Use spray adhesive to adhere the top edge of the triangles to the backside of the paper strip. Stitch this garland to the right side of the front piece of the circle paper. Cut a piece of white paper into a small rectangle and write "thanks!" or other message and stitch this onto the circle, right below the paper garland.
- **Ghost:** When stitching, leave open the top portion of the ghost. Glue the two eyes to the front of the pouch and draw a circle for the mouth with the black marker Ⓒ. Let dry. Insert candy into the ghost and sew the opening closed.

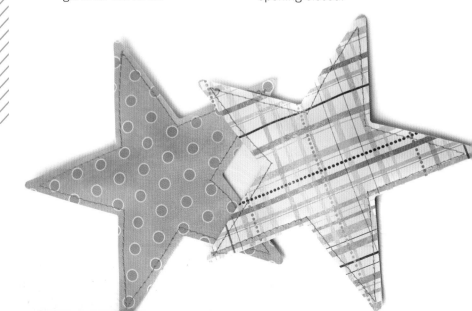

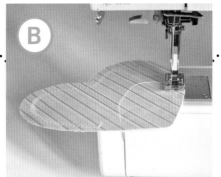

## cheri's Tips

- Use the pouches as stocking stuffers, party favors, Valentine's Day gifts, and more!
- Embellish the pouches with stickers, tape, and doodles.

hello!

love you.

thanks!

# DRAWSTRING GAME BOARD

**Designer:** MEGAN HUNT

Take this game board on the road to keep little ones entertained and organized. Once they are done playing either checkers or tic-tac-toe, they can keep all of their pieces in the drawstring bag!

## Gather

- Basic Machine-Sewing Tool Kit (page 13)
- ½ yard (.5 m) beige felt
- ½ yard (.5 m) brown felt
- ¼ yard (.2 m) light green felt
- ¼ yard (.2 m) pink felt
- 1 piece of gray felt, 9 x 12 inches (22.9 x 30.5 cm)
- Fabric glue
- 1 package of seam binding, ½-inch (1.3 mm) wide
- 1 package of seam binding, 2-inch (5.1 cm) wide
- Safety pin

**Finished Dimensions:**

12 inches (30.5 cm) square

**Seam Allowance:**

½ inch (1.3 cm)

## Make

**1** From the beige and brown felt, cut one square each that measures 13 x 14 inches (33 x 35.6 cm); these are the front and back sides of the game board/bag. Then cut the light green, pink, and gray felt into the following sizes:

- 9 light green pieces, each 3 inches (7.6 cm) square
- 32 light green pieces, each 1½ inches (3.8 cm) square
- 9 pink pieces, each 3 inches (7.6 cm) square
- 12 pink pieces, each 1½ inches (3.8 cm) square
- 12 gray pieces, each 1½ inches (3.8 cm) square

**2** Checkerboard markers: Freehand-cut each of the 12 pink and 12 gray 1½-inch (3.8 cm) squares into circles Ⓐ (see next page).

**3** Tic-tac-toe markers: Use fabric glue to adhere one of the light green 3-inch (7.6 cm) squares to one of the pink 3-inch (7.6 cm) squares. Repeat with the other same-size squares until you have nine that are pink on one side and light green on the other side.

**4** Make the checkerboard side of the board/bag:

- Fold under one short side of the beige felt piece by 1½ inches (3.8 cm) and press. This will be the top of the bag. Lay this piece on a work surface with the folded side facing down.
- Being mindful of a ½ inch (1.3 cm) seam allowance on the sides and bottom, lay the 32 light green felt squares onto the beige felt piece in a checkerboard pattern.
- One square at a time, secure each square with a dab of fabric glue.
- Machine-stitch straight lines across each row and column of squares to secure the edges of the squares. You're basically sewing a grid, with each square outlined by stitching Ⓑ (see next page).

**5** Make the tic-tac-toe side of the board/bag:

- Fold under one short side of the brown felt piece 1½ inches (3.8 cm) and press. This will be the top of the bag. Lay this piece on a work surface with the folded side facing down.
- Cut the ½-inch (1.3 cm) seam binding into four 13-inch (33 cm) pieces. Lay two of these pieces onto the brown felt horizontally and the other two pieces vertically, to make a tic-tac-toe grid. Pin and sew in place ⓒ.

**6** Assemble the bag:

- With right sides facing, pin the beige and brown felt pieces together. Stitch up one of the sides. When you get to the top 1½-inch (3.8 cm) portion that was folded down in step 4, unfold and continue stitching up the side.
- Create the drawstring channel by refolding the top portion down and stitching all along the folded edge, as close to the raw edge as possible.
- Stitch across the bottom and up the remaining side, stopping at the edge of the channel.
- Turn the bag right side out.
- Attach a safety pin to the end of the 2-inch (5.1 cm) wide seam binding and pull it through the entire channel.

*megan's*
# Tips

- Instead of felt circles, use buttons in two different colors for checker pieces.

- Leave the tic-tac-toe squares as is or have your child use a marker or rubber stamps to make Xs and Os on the pieces.

- Use ribbons or fabric strips instead of seam binding for the tic-tac-toe game board and the drawstring for the bag.

- The body of the bag can also be made with an old non-patterned towel that you cut up.

A

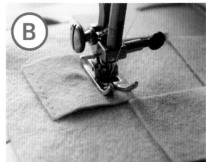

B

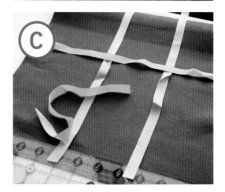

C

# PENNANT NAME BANNER

**Designer:** CYNTHIA SHAFFER

With each pennant made from felt, this banner hangs nicely on a wall without any part of it sagging or puckering. What a great way to brighten up a child's room and make them feel special!

# Gather

- Basic Machine-Sewing Tool Kit (page 13)
- 1 sheet of cardstock
- Black marker
- ⅓ yard (.3 m) gold felt
- Red thread
- ¼ yard (.2 m) paper-backed fusible web
- ¼ yard (.2 m) red patterned cotton fabric
- Perle cotton (size 5), 1 skein of white
- Small pompoms: 15 white and 10 light green
- White glue
- 1½ yards (1.4 m) of ½-inch (1.3 cm) wide white ribbon
- Safety pin

**Finished Dimensions:**

Each pennant is 6 x 10 inches (15.2 x 25.4 cm); the assembled banner is 33 x 10 inches (83.8 x 25.4 cm)

# Make

**1** Create a template by cutting the cardstock to measure 6 x 11 inches (15.2 x 27.9 cm). Trace the template onto the gold felt five times with a black marker.

**2** Use pinking shears to cut out the five traced rectangles.

**3** Prepare each pennant as follows:
- Fold one of the gold felt rectangles in half lengthwise and press lightly. Place a pin at the bottom of the rectangle at the fold.
- Fold the right lower corner up and in toward the pressed center crease and pin in place. Repeat for the left corner Ⓐ.
- Fold the top of the rectangle down 1 inch (2.5 cm), press and then pin in place.
- Using red thread, machine stitch across the top and the bottom of the gold felt panel, catching the corners that have been folded up, and removing pins as you go Ⓑ.

**4** To finish the pennants:
- Cut the paper-backed fusible web into five 5½-inch (14 cm) squares.
- Use a pencil to lightly draw one of the letters for the name on the non-paper side of the fusible web piece, freeform style. Fill the square as much as possible.
- Flip the fusible web over to the paper side and trace over your lightly-drawn letter. This process of tracing over the letter a second time will ensure that the final fused letters are oriented correctly.
- Repeat for all the remaining letters in the name.

**5** Cut the red patterned cotton fabric into five 5½-inch (14 cm) squares.

**6** Following the manufacturer's directions, press the fusible web for each letter to the wrong side of the red patterned fabric square.

**7** Cut out the fused letter and then peel off the paper backing. Center the letter on the gold felt and fuse in place with a hot iron Ⓒ.

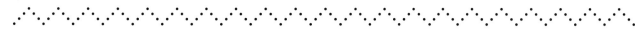

**8** Hand-sew around each letter with a running stitch, using white perle cotton and a hand-sewing needle Ⓓ.

**9** Place a pin at the center of each lower red-stitched line. Glue the pompoms onto the gold felt, centering the first one onto where the pin is, and then adding four more, alternating white and green. Let the glue dry Ⓔ.

**10** Knot the end of the white ribbon and push the safety pin into the knot. Thread the safety pin through the top channels of all the pennants. Center the banner on the ribbon. Knot the ends of the ribbon close to the first and last pennant Ⓕ.

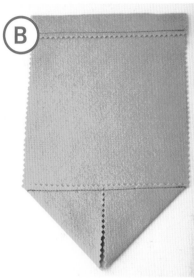

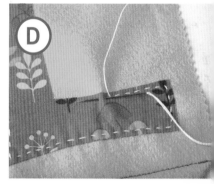

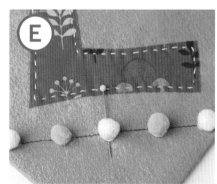

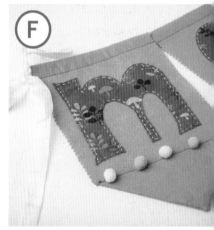

## cynthia's Tips

The hand-sewing around the letters is just for added decoration. If you prefer, skip that portion to save time!

**Designer:** HEATHER JONES

Thirty small squares of fabric and one large rectangle of chenille are all you need to make this pretty quilt that will be loved and treasured for years to come.

# Gather

- Basic Macine-Sewing Tool Kit (page 13)
- ⅓ yard (.3 m) each of ten different quilting cotton fabrics, at least 42 inches (106.7 cm) wide
- 1¾ yards (1.6 m) cotton chenille fabric, 54 inches (137.2 cm) wide
- Perle cotton (size 5), 1 skein of cream

### Finished Dimensions:

50 x 60 inches
(127 x 152.4 cm)

### Seam allowance:

¼ inch (6 mm) for patchwork top, ½ inch (1.3 cm) for sewing the top and back together

# Make

**1** Using a rotary cutter, quilting ruler, and cutting mat, cut the yardage of each of the quilting cottons as follows:
- Cut a strip that measures 10½ inches x WOF (26.7 cm x width of fabric).
- Sub-cut the strip into three 10½-inch (26.7 cm) squares.

**2** Arrange the fabric squares to create a design that you like. You will be creating six rows made up of five squares per row.

**3** Construct the top row, going left to right, by machine-stitching the first two squares with right sides together. Stitch the next square to the first piece with right sides together.

**4** Repeat Step 3 to construct the other five rows.

**5** Press the seams as follows:
- Rows 1, 3, and 5: to the right
- Rows 2, 4, and 6: to the left

**6** With right sides together, sew Row 1 to Row 2, matching up the seams between the squares of each row. Since they were pressed in opposite directions, they should lock together.

**7** Sew Row 3 to the pieced section, right sides together. Sew Rows 4, 5, and 6 in the same manner to complete the patchwork top. Press open all seams between the rows.

**8** To make the chenille backing, cut the yardage to measure 60½ inches x WOF (153.7 cm x width of fabric) piece. Cut off the selvages and then cut the chenille lengthwise so that it measures 50½ inches x WOF (128.3 cm x width of fabric).

**9** With right sides together, place the patchwork top onto the chenille, and pin. Be sure to use lots of pins, as chenille is much thicker than the quilting-weight fabrics and has a tendency to slip around, especially while sewing.

**10** Using a ½ inch (1.3 cm) seam allowance, stitch along the perimeter of the throw, leaving a 12-inch (30.5 cm) opening. Backstitch at the beginning and end of this seam to lock the stitches. Remove the pins as you sew. Carefully trim off the excess fabric at the seam allowances of each of the four corners, making sure not to snip the threads of the seams.

**11** Turn the throw right side out, gently pulling it through the opening. Use a pencil or stuffing tool to gently push out each of the four corners.

**12** Turn under the seam allowances at the opening. Press and pin closed. Topstitch along the entire perimeter of the throw, starting at the opening. Backstitch at the end of the seam to lock the stitches Ⓐ.

**13** Thread a hand-sewing needle with perle cotton but do not knot the end. At the intersection of any four squares of the quilt top, make

a tied knot as follows:

- Insert the needle through the top, very close to the intersection through all thicknesses until about 4 inches (10.2 cm) of perle cotton is left at the top of the patchwork.
- Bring the needle back up through all layers, very close to the first hole Ⓑ.
- Make a double knot with the two strands of perle cotton and snip the strands to about ½ inch (6 mm) from the knot Ⓒ Ⓓ.
- Repeat at all remaining intersecting squares.

## *heather's* Tips

- Use your stash fabric for this project and adjust the size of the squares to make the throw bigger or smaller.

- Clothes that your child has outgrown can also be used, as long as you can cut enough squares in the same size. It's a great way to remember T-shirts and other garments from the past.

# NESTING DOLLS

**Designer:** JOEL HENRIQUES AND JENNY DOH

Your kids will enjoy these dolls designed to stand up, lay down, or even become puppets. Once playtime is over, you'll love how they all fit nicely inside one another, from large, medium, small, to miniature.

# Gather

- Basic Machine-Sewing Tool Kit (page 13)
- ¼ yard (.2 m) cotton duck fabric
- Felt or fleece scraps in blue, red, yellow, and black (or other colors you have in your stash)
- Fabric markers
- Hair dryer

## Finished Dimensions

Large doll: 5½ x 9 inches (14 x 22.9 cm)

Medium doll: 4½ x 8 inches (11.4 x 20.3 cm)

Small doll: 4 x 7 inches (10.2 x 17.8 cm)

Miniature doll: 3¼ x 6 inches (8.3 x 15.2 cm)

## Seam allowance:

¼ inch (6 mm)

# Make

**1** Cut the cotton duck and felt into rectangles as follows:
- Large: Cut one square each of cotton and felt, 6 x 9½ inches (15.2 x 24.1 cm)
- Medium: Cut one square each of cotton and felt, 5 x 8½ inches (12.7 x 21.6 cm)
- Small: Cut one square each of cotton and felt, 4½ x 7½ inches (11.4 x 19 cm)
- Miniature: Cut one square each of cotton and felt, 3¾ x 6½ inches (9.5 x 16.5 cm)

**Note:** Try to cut the cotton duck so that one of the short sides is on the selvage. Because it won't fray, you can position that edge at the bottom of each doll and skip stitching it. If you are unable to cut it on the selvage, turn one of the short sides of each cotton duck piece by ¼ inch (6 mm) and stitch.

**2** Make the doll sleeves:

- With right sides together, place the large cotton duck piece on top of the large felt piece, with the bottom short edges aligned.
- Use a water-soluble marker to draw a curve at the top left and right corner as sewing guides.
- Stitch around the edges of the sides and top, leaving the bottom edge open.
- Trim the seam close to the stitching Ⓐ and turn right side out.
- Repeat the process for the remaining dolls.

**3** Use fabric markers to draw a figure on the cotton duck side of the doll Ⓑ. Use a hair dryer on the highest heat setting to blow-dry the ink to ensure permanence.

## *joel and jenny's* Tips

- If your child is old enough, encourage him or her to make the drawings on the dolls and celebrate any small imperfections that may result.

- If your child is not old enough, you could make the drawings inspired by your child's drawings or inspired by other characters that your child likes from favorite books or stories.

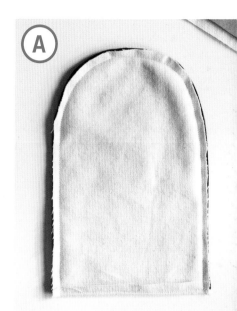

Ⓐ

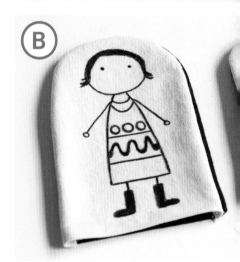

Ⓑ

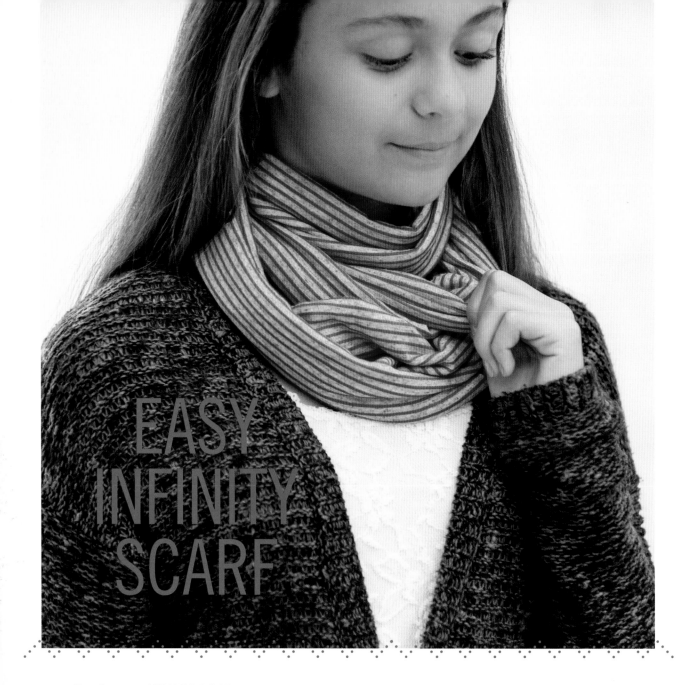

**Designer:** JENNY DOH

Start with just a half-yard of lightweight knit fabric and you won't need to do any additional cutting for this project. It's so simple to create, you may want to make several to coordinate with your entire wardrobe.

## Gather

- Basic Machine-Sewing Tool Kit (page 13)
- ½ yard (.5 m) 44-inch (1.2 m) cm) wide, red-striped lightweight knit fabric (or other color and pattern of your choice)

**Finished Dimensions:**

43 inches (109.2 cm) circumference x 17 inches (43.2 cm)

**Seam Allowance:**

½ inch (1.3 cm)

### jenny's Tip

Wear the scarf as a long single loop around your neck, or wear it shorter by wrapping the scarf once, twice, or even a third time around your neck. The knit fabric will cause a nice draping effect at any length.

## Make

**1** With right sides facing, fold the fabric in half with long sides together. Pin the long sides together and machine stitch Ⓐ.

**2** Turn the piece right side out.

**3** Fold the sewn piece in half so that the open short ends are together. Lift the top layer only, twist it 180 degrees, and put it back down so that the open short ends are again aligned Ⓑ.

**4** Grab the two layers that are right sides together with your thumb and index finger, and carefully put these layers in your sewing machine and start sewing Ⓒ. Continue sewing along the layers until you are approximately 3 inches (7.6 cm) from where you started.

**5** Take the fabric out of the machine. You will have a stitched tube (with a twist) and a small opening. Use a hand-sewing needle and thread to whipstitch the opening closed Ⓓ.

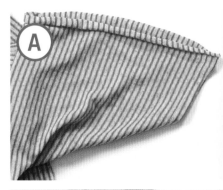

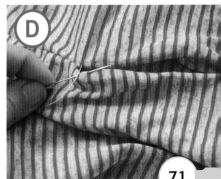

# MONOGRAM PILLOW

**Designer:** SUSAN PHILLIPS

With just a straight machine stitch and a simple hand stitch, your kid can make this groovy pillow for the bedroom or the play room.

## Gather

- Basic Machine-Sewing Tool Kit (page 13)
- Monogram templates (pages 121–122)
- ⅔ yard (.6 m) printed cotton twill
- ⅓ yard (.3 m) cream cotton twill
- 10-inch (25.4 cm) diameter dinner plate for circle template
- ¼ yard (.2 m) or large scrap of fuchsia felt
- 6-strand embroidery floss, 1 skein of lime green
- 18-inch (45.7 cm) square pillow form

**Finished Dimensions:**

18 inches (45.7 cm) square

**Seam allowance:**

½ inch (1.3 cm)

## Make

**1** Cut the printed cotton twill into the following pieces
- Front: Cut 1 19-inch (48.3 cm) square
- Back: Cut 2 19 x 13 inches (48.3 x 33 cm)

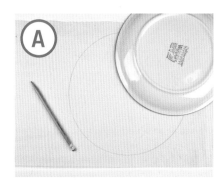

**2** Place the dinner plate on the wrong side of the cream fabric and trace around the plate using a pencil. Cut out the circle Ⓐ.

**3** Select the letter you want to use from the templates, and size it to be approximately 7 to 8 inches (17.8 to 20.3 cm) tall. Cut out the letter, pin it onto the felt, and carefully cut the felt Ⓑ.

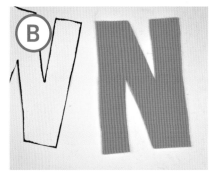

**4** Pin the felt letter in the center of the cut circle fabric. Machine-stitch along all edges of the letter Ⓒ.

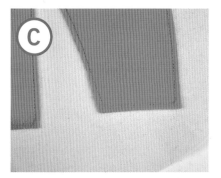

**5** Center and pin the wrong side of the circle to the right side of the pillow front. Machine-stitch the circle to the square ¼ inch (6 mm) from the edge of the circle Ⓓ.

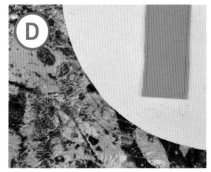

**6** With a hand-sewing needle and embroidery floss, add a running stitch directly over the machine stitches from step 5 Ⓔ.

**7** To prepare the back pieces, make a 1-inch (2.5 cm) double-fold hem on one long side of both pieces Ⓕ.

**8** Assemble the pillow:
- Place the pillow front on your work surface, right side facing up.
- Pin one back piece in place, aligning the long raw side with the top edge of the front and aligning raw edges on both sides Ⓖ.
- Pin the remaining back in place, aligning the long raw side with the bottom edge of the front and aligning raw edges on both sides. The hemmed edges will overlap in the center of the pillow.
- Stitch along all four sides of the entire square and trim the corners Ⓗ.
- Turn right side out.

**9** Stuff the monogrammed pillow with a pillow form.

## susan's Tips

- Instead of machine-stitching the letter onto the circle, use embroidery floss and hand-sew it on.

- Reverse-appliqué the letter by making the felt into a circle, and placing that circle beneath the cream colored circle. Trace the letter onto the cream colored circle with a water-soluble marker, stitch along all edges of the letter and then cut away the portion of the cream fabric within the sewn letter to reveal the felt underneath.

- Instead of appliqué, create a stencil of the letter with heavy paper or light cardboard from an empty cereal box. Use the stencil and fabric paint to paint on the letter.

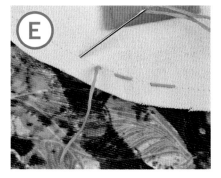

RACCOON SWEATSHIRT

**Designer:** MARY RASCH

This raccoon hoodie is so cute and comfortable, it'll be enjoyed year-round. The templates will work with assorted sweatshirt sizes, so there is no need to adjust them.

# Gather

- Basic Machine-Sewing Tool Kit (page 13)
- Raccoon templates (page 118)
- Brown hooded sweatshirt
- ¼ yard (.2 m) brown fleece
- ¼ yard (.2 m) black fleece
- ¼ yard (.2 m) white fleece
- Threads to match the felt pieces
- 2 black beads for eyes, 6 or 8 mm
- 1 black rounded bead for nose, ½ inch (1.3 cm) in diameter

**Finished Dimensions:**

A child's size small was used for this project

Seam allowance: ¼ inch (6 mm)

# Make

**1** Enlarge and use the templates to cut the following pieces:

- Template A (outer eye): Cut 2 (mirrored pair) from white fleece
- Template B (inner eye): Cut 2 (mirrored pair) from black fleece
- Template C (outer ear): Cut 2 from brown fleece
- Template C (outer ear): Cut 2 from white fleece
- Template D (inner ear): Cut 2 from brown fleece
- Template E (tail): Cut 2 (mirrored pair) from brown fleece
- Templates F, G, and H (tail stripes): Cut 2 of each (mirrored pair) from black fleece

**2** To create the eyes:

- Pin the white outer eye pieces onto the top of the hoodie with one straight side along the front binding and the other approximately 1 inch (2.5 cm) from the top center seam of the hood. Refer to the photo for guidance. Hand-sew the pieces in place Ⓐ.
- Pin the black inner eye pieces on top of the sewn outer eye piece with straight sides aligned. Hand-sew in place Ⓑ.
- Hand-sew one of the small black beads to the inner corner of the eye, approximately ¾ inch (1.9 cm) from both straight sides Ⓒ.

**3** To create the ears.

- Center and pin each inner ear piece on top of a white outer ear piece, with straight edges aligned. Machine-stitch around the curved edge of the inner ear.
- With right sides together, pin each stitched piece to a brown outer ear piece along the curved edge, leaving the straight edge open. Stitch and then flip right side out.
- Fold each ear in half along the straight edge and hand-sew through all thicknesses Ⓓ. Hand-sew the ear onto the sides of the hood, approximately 3 inches (7.6 cm) from the center seam of the hood and ½ inch (1.3 cm) above the eye Ⓔ.

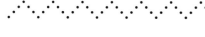

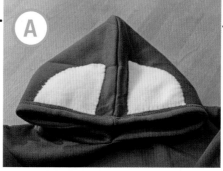

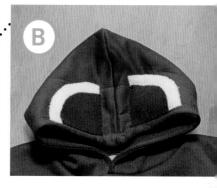

**4** To create the tail:

- Pin a set of black tail stripes onto one of the brown tail pieces and machine-stitch. Repeat for the second set of stripes and other brown tail piece.
- With right sides together, pin and stitch both curved sides of the tail, leaving the straight edge open.
- Trim the seam allowances as needed and turn right side out through the opening.
- Center and pin the tail to the lower back portion of the hoodie, along the top of the waistband. Hand-sew in place **F**.

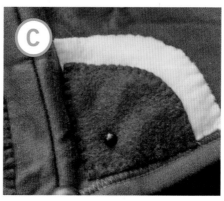

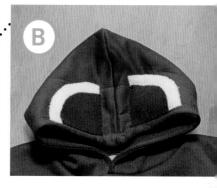

## *mary's* Tip

Instead of using a brown sweatshirt and fleece, you can choose a gray color. The tail is not stuffed to provide comfort to the child wearing the sweatshirt when sitting down. However, if that is not a concern, feel free to fill the tail with stuffing before attaching it to the sweatshirt.

# COZY PILLOW LOUNGE

**Designer:** JAMEY EKINS

Sew up two large pieces of fabric with a few straight stitches and stuff it with four standard-sized pillows. Who knew a cozy lounge could be this simple?

## Gather

- Basic Machine-Sewing Tool Kit (page 13)
- 2¼ yards (2 m) blue patterned flannel
- 2¼ yards (2 m) blue and pink patterned flannel
- 4 standard-sized pillows

**Finished Dimensions:**

33 x 73 inches (83.8 x 185.4 cm)

**Seam Allowance:**

½ inch (1.3 cm)

### jamey's Tips

- Cut up flat, cotton bed sheets to make a fun cover to use during warmer summer days.
- Adjust the size of the lounge to accommodate extra large or extra small pillows.

## Make

**1** Using a rotary cutter, quilter's ruler, and a cutting mat, cut the yardage of both flannels to measure 34½ x 33 inches (87.6 x 83.8 cm).

**2** Pin the flannel pieces with right sides together. Machine-stitch one short side, one long side, and the other short side, removing pins as you go. Trim the stitched corners with scissors and turn right side out Ⓐ.

**3** Make a ½-inch (1.3 cm) double-fold hem along the entire open raw edge Ⓑ.

**4** Use a water-soluble marker to mark a line 18 inches (45.7 cm) down from the top seam (one of the short sides) Ⓒ. Make two more lines below it, 18 inches (45.7 cm) apart. Stitch along each line to make four pillow pockets Ⓓ. Insert a pillow into each pocket.

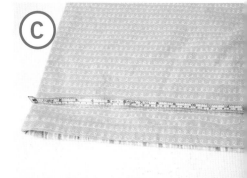

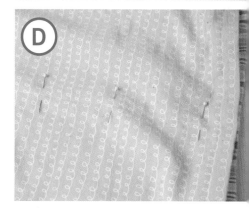

# PLAYHOUSE

**Designer:** CYNTHIA SHAFFER

Your kids will use and treasure this magnificent playhouse for years. Because it fits over a standard small card table, it can be disassembled, folded, and put away when the playhouse is not in use.

# Gather

- Basic Machine-Sewing Tool Kit (page 13)
- Shingle template (page 115)
- 4 yards (3.7 m) turquoise patterned cotton fabric
- 1 yard (.9 m) green patterned fabric
- ¾ yard (.7 m) gray felt
- ¾ yard (.7 m) orange patterned cotton fabric
- ¾ yard (.7 m) fuchsia patterned cotton fabric
- 4 yards (3.7 m) 1-inch (2.5 cm) lime green ribbon
- Light turquoise thread
- Small, standard-sized card table, 34 inches (86.4 cm) square and 28 inches (71.1 cm) high

### Finished Dimensions:

34 inches (86.4 cm) square and 28 inches (71.1 cm) high

### Seam Allowance:

½ inch (1.3 cm)

- Top and bottom of windows: Cut four pieces from gray felt, 11¼ x 1¾ inches (28.6 x 4.4 cm)
- Sides of windows: Cut four pieces from gray felt: 1¾ x 10¾ inches (4.4 x 27.3 cm)
- Vertical strip in window: Cut two pieces from gray felt, ¾ x 10¾ inches (1.9 x 27.3 cm)
- Horizontal strip in window: Cut two pieces from gray felt, ¾ x 9 inches (1.9 x 22.9 cm)
- Window shades: Cut two pieces from orange cotton, 11½ x 24 inches (29.2 x 61 cm)
- Door curtains: Cut two pieces from fuchsia cotton, 13 x 22½ inches (33 x 57.2 cm)

# Make

## CUT OUT THE PIECES

**1** Use the rotary cutter, quilting ruler, and cutting mat to cut the following pieces. For the gray felt strips, cut along the outermost edges to allow for cutting 24 shingles from the template (in step 9):

- Sides of playhouse: Cut four panels from the turquoise cotton, 35 x 29 inches (88.9 x 73.7 cm)
- Roof: Cut one piece from patterned green cotton, 35 inches (88.9 cm) square
- Top of door: Cut one piece from gray felt, 14½ x 2¼ inches (36.8 x 5.7 cm)
- Sides of door: Cut two pieces from gray felt: 2¼ x 21¼ inches (5.7 x 54 cm)

## ASSEMBLE THE FRONT WINDOW

**2** Lay one of the turquoise panels on a flat surface. This panel will be the front of the playhouse. Pin the gray felt window strips as follows:

- Top strip: 8 inches (20.3 cm) down from the top and 3 inches (7.6 cm) from the left side.
- Sides: parallel to the sides of the front panel; tuck the top ½ inch (1.3 cm) of both sides under the lower edge of the top strip.

- Bottom strip: parallel to the top, overlapping the bottom of the side strips by ½ inch (1.3 cm).
- Vertical strip: center inside the window, tucking the ends under the top and bottom frame strips.
- Horizontal strip: center inside the window: tucking the ends under the side strips Ⓐ.

## COMPLETE THE FRONT WINDOW

**3** Stitch all sides of all felt pieces, getting as close to the felt edges as possible Ⓑ.
- Flip the panel to the wrong side and carefully cut away the turquoise fabric inside the windowpanes Ⓒ.

## ASSEMBLE THE DOOR FRAME

**4** On the right side of the front panel, pin the gray felt strips as follows:
- Top of the door: 6 inches (15.2 cm) down from the top and 3 inches (7.6 cm) from the right side.
- Sides of door: parallel to the sides of the front panel; tuck the top ½ inch (1.3 cm) of both sides under the lower edge of the top strip.

## COMPLETE THE DOOR

**5** Stitch all sides of all felt pieces, getting as close to the felt edges as possible.
- Flip the panel to the backside and cut the turquoise fabric away from the inside of the doorframe, close to the gray felt.

## MAKE THE SECOND WINDOW

**6** Lay another turquoise panel on a flat surface. This panel will be the right side of the playhouse. Repeat steps 2 and 3 for this window, except center the window in the panel, 8 inches (20.3 cm) down from the top.

## MAKE THE WINDOW CURTAINS

**7** For each curtain, do the following:
- With right sides facing, fold an orange cotton piece, with short ends aligned (forming a shape that is almost square) Ⓓ. Pin and sew the long sides together, leaving the short ends open. Turn right side out.
- Cut 2 lengths of green ribbon that measure 22 inches (55.9 cm) each. Fold one piece of the ribbon in half to find the center and then pin the center of the ribbon to the top of the

window frame. Repeat with the other ribbon. Baste the ribbons in place.
- Pin the raw edge of the window shade to the top of the window frame as shown, on top of the stitched ribbons. Stitch in place, backstitching at the beginning and the end of the seam Ⓔ.

## MAKE THE DOOR CURTAIN

**8** Make two curtain panels from the fuchsia fabric as follows:
- Make two rows of gathering stitches at the top of both curtains by machine-basting ½ inch (1.3 cm) from the top edge of the panel, backstitching at the start; repeat stitching ¼ inch (6 mm) from the top edge of each panel, backstitching at the start Ⓕ.
- Pull the non-backstitched threads of the basting stitch on the wrong side of the panel to gather the curtain, securing the excess thread ends onto a pin as you are pulling them.
- On the wrong side of the door opening, pin the curtain panels side-by-side, overlapping the top gathered edges by 1 inch (2.5 cm) in the top center of the doorframe Ⓖ.

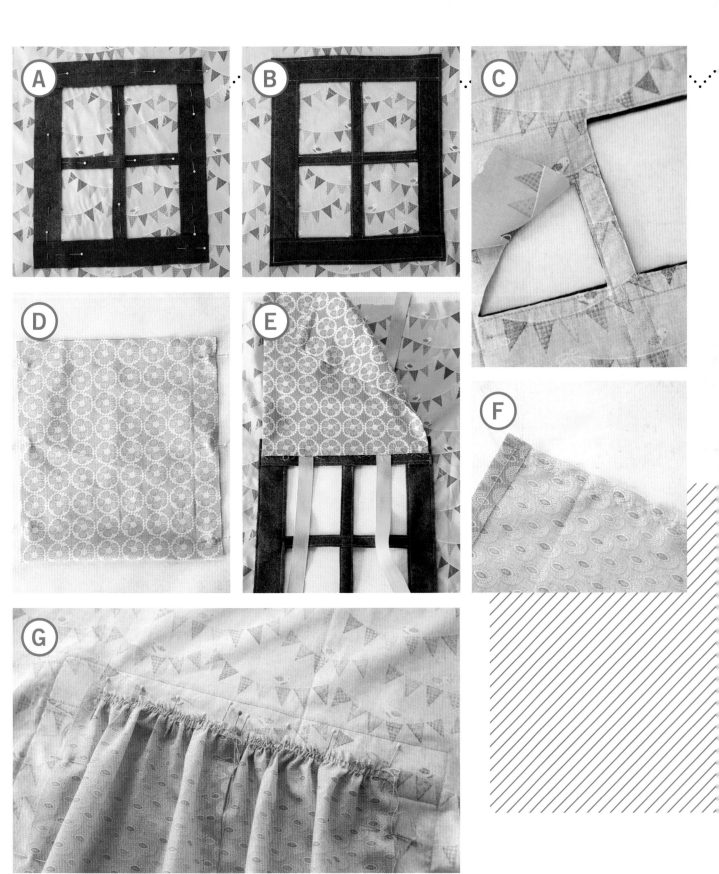

- Pin the right and left sides of the curtain to the door frames from top to bottom 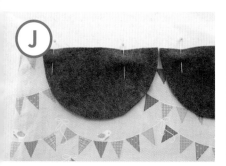 (H). The curtain will be about 1¼ inches (3.2 cm) short of the bottom edge of the playhouse.
- Machine stitch the curtains in place on the sides and across the top.
- To make the ties, cut four lengths of ribbon that each measure 14 inches (35.6 cm) long. Turn under one short end of two of the ribbons and pin them to the door frame on both sides of the curtain 10 inches (25.4 cm) down from the top of the doorframe. Repeat with

the remaining ribbons on the opposite side of the door (I).

## MAKE THE SHINGLES

9 Use the template and trace 24 scallop shingles with the gray felt. Pin the shingles to the top edge of the turquoise panels (six on each side) and machine-baste in place (J).

## ASSEMBLE THE PLAYHOUSE

10 With right sides together, pin the short edges of the turquoise panels together. Repeat until all four panels are pinned together.
- Machine-stitch the panels together, starting ½ inch

(1.3 cm) from the top edge. Backstitch at the beginning and at the end of the seam.
- Pin one top edge of the turquoise fabric to one edge of the green roof square. Start stitching ½ inch (1.3 cm) from the edge, and then stitch to within ½ inch (1.3 cm) of the opposite edge, backstitching at both ends (K). Repeat for the remaining three sides.
- Turn under the bottom edge of the playhouse ¼ inch (6 mm) and then another 1 inch (2.5 cm). Stitch the hem in place.

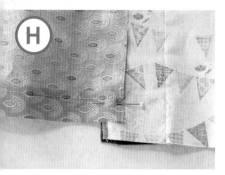

## cynthia's Tips

- To simplify the project, leave off the window shades and the door curtains.
- For more visibility, add windows to all sides of the playhouse.

# HIP HIP HOORAY
## PROJECT BELT

**Designer:** KATHLEEN WALCK

This project can be made with almost any outgrown or upcycled pair of pants. Depending on the age and skill of the child, he or she could participate in different ways, from embroidering the pockets, tracing the lining fabric, or sewing the pieces together.

# Gather

- Basic Machine-Sewing Tool Kit (page 13)
- 1 pair of gray corduroy pants with pockets and belt loops
- ½ yard (.5 m) cotton fabric for the lining
- 1 fat quarter cotton fabric for the belt
- 6-strand embroidery floss, 1 skein each teal and orange (or other coordinating colors)

**Finished Dimensions:**

This apron was made with a size 2T pair of pants, resulting in a final apron that measures 18 x 8 inches (45.7 x 20.3 cm)

**Seam Allowance:**

¼ inch (6 mm) and ½ inch (1.3 cm) as noted

# Make

**1** Use a quilter's ruler, rotary cutter, and cutting mat to cut the legs off of the pants, being careful not to cut into the pockets. Try to leave about 1 inch (2.5 cm) below the pockets if you can. Carefully cut away the zipper, making sure not to cut into the pockets Ⓐ.

**2** Pin the cut pants onto the lining fabric, wrong sides together. Trace the outline of the pants with a water-soluble marker. Cut out the fabric along the traced lines Ⓑ. Remove pins.

**3** Pin the cut pants and lining with right sides together Ⓒ. Machine-stitch the layers with a ¼ inch (6 mm) seam allowance, starting at the top of one side at the bottom of the pant's waistband, backstitching, then stitching down that side, along the bottom, and up the other side, stopping at the bottom of the waistband. Take care not to catch the pockets in your stitching. Trim excess fabric from the corners and edges Ⓓ.

**4** Turn the project right side out and press (E).

**5** Turn under the lining fabric along the top edge, keeping the top edge aligned with the bottom of the waistband. Press and pin (F).

**6** Whipstitch the top seam closed with a hand-sewing needle and thread, making sure to stitch only through the top layer of the waistband fabric to prevent sewing the belt loops closed. Whipstitch closed the edges of the waistband as well (G).

**7** Use a water-soluble marker to draw your child's initials onto each front pocket. Use embroidery floss to backstitch along the traced letters.

**8** To make the belt:
- Cut the fat quarter into two 4 x 18-inch (10.2 x 45.7 cm) strips (or three strips for a larger/older child).
- With right sides facing, join two strips by pinning and stitching two short ends together. For a larger/older child, join a third strip; then try it out on the child. You want the length to go around the waist or hips, with enough extra for tying. Trim any excess fabric as needed.
- Fold under the fabric ½ inch (1.3 cm) at each short end, then press and stitch.
- Press and fold the strip as for double-fold bias tape: Press in half along the length, open and press both long edges toward the center fold, then refold along the center and press again (H).
- Stitch along ends and long open edges to complete the belt.
- Thread the belt through the belt loops with the ends in the back for tying (I).

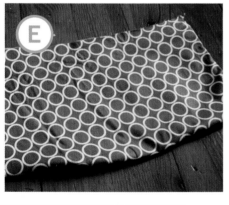

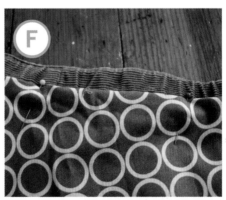

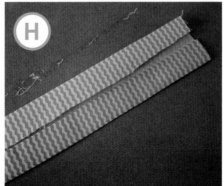

## kathleen's Tip

Use the extra fabric from the cut-off legs to add extra loops or additional pockets to the project belt.

SIMPLE
A-LINE
SKIRT

**Designer:** CAL PATCH

## Gather

- Basic Machine-Sewing Tool Kit (page 13)
- Skirt templates (page 124–125)
- ¾ yard (.7 m) of cotton denim
- 1 yard (.9 m) of elastic, ¼-inch (6 mm) wide
- 2 pieces of felt fabric in contrasting colors, 5 x 7 inches (12.7 x 17.8 cm)

### Finished Dimensions:

Small: 21-inch (53.3 cm) waist and 10½ inch (26.7 cm) length

Medium: 23-inch (58.4 cm) waist and 11 inch (27.9 cm) length

Large: 25-inch (63.5 cm) waist and 11½ inch (29.2 cm) length

### Seam allowance:

½ inch (1.3 cm)

Sometimes, you may prefer the more muted "wrong" side of denim. That's exactly how I felt about this denim and so I designated the "wrong" side as my "right" side, resulting in a lighter-colored skirt.

## Make

**1** *Note:* In these instructions, the lighter side of the denim fabric is considered the "right" side. Enlarge and use templates to cut the following pieces. All templates already include seam allowance.

- Template A (front and back): Cut 2 from denim on the fold
- Template B (waistband): Cut 1 from denim on the fold
- Template C (apple appliqué): Cut 1 from red felt
- Templates D and E (chevron accents): Cut 1 each from white felt

**2** Pin the front and back pieces together, with right sides facing. Machine-stitch both side seams. To finish the raw edges and prevent them from fraying when the skirt is washed, run a zigzag stitch along the raw edges through both thicknesses.

**3** Make the waistband as follows:

- Pin the short ends of the waistband piece with right sides facing and machine-stitch. Press the seam open.
- Measure the child's waist and cut the elastic to that measurement.
- Without twisting, overlap the two ends of the elastic by 1 inch (2.5 cm) and stitch together. *Note:* It may be easier to stitch this by hand as some machines will have trouble grasping the narrow elastic layers. Just be sure the ends are securely connected, even if it's not pretty, since it'll be hidden inside the waistband.
- Lay the joined elastic loop on top of the waistband, with the wrong side of the waistband and the wrong side of the pressed open seam facing you.

- Fold the waistband in half with wrong sides facing, causing the elastic to become encased. Pin along the entire raw edges of the waistband until the elastic is encased Ⓐ.
- Zigzag stitch the raw edges of the waistband to seal in the elastic. *Note:* The elastic will cause the waistband to gather up as you sew, but just keep pulling to flatten out the part you are sewing, and let the rest of it gather up as you go.

**4** To attach the waistband, pin it evenly around the top edge of the skirt, with right sides together, lining up the zigzagged waistband edge with the raw top edge of the skirt and sew Ⓑ. Stretch the waistband as you work so that the fabric layers are flat as you sew over them. After you sew the seam, zigzag stitch over the raw edges to prevent fraying.

**5** To make the hem, trim the corners of the seam allowance at the bottom of each side seam. Make a double-fold hem by turning up the bottom edge ½ inch (1.3 cm) then another ½ inch (1.3 cm). Pin and press. From the wrong side of the skirt, carefully and evenly stitch along the folded hem Ⓒ.

**6** Turn skirt right side out and place the appliqué onto the front where you want it. Use embroidery floss and straight stitch it down. Attach the chevron appliqués on top of the apple and stitch them down with straight stitches.

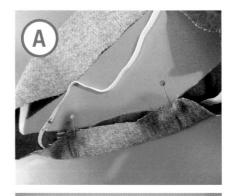

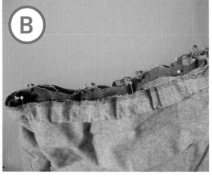

## cal's Tips

- Try different appliqué shapes with different colors of felt or fabric.
- Create a small pocket patch with contrasting fabric or remove a small pocket from an old pair of jeans and appliqué that onto the skirt.

# TERRIFIC TUNIC

**Designer:** NICOLE BLUM

Depending on the length of the T-shirt you work with, you can make this into a tunic or a dress.

# Gather

- Basic Hand-Sewing Tool Kit (page 9)
- Crewneck graphic T-shirt*
- 6-strand embroidery floss: less than one skein each of colors that coordinate with your T-shirt
- 1 yard (.9 m) of fold-over elastic, ½-inch (1.3 cm) wide
- Safety pin

*A woman's large will fit younger kids and a men's small will fit older kids. Just make sure that the T-shirt you select doesn't have unusually large armholes.*

# Make

**1** Cut the T-shirt:
- Fold the T-shirt in half, matching up the sleeves and side.
- Place the ruler horizontally across the upper part of the folded T-shirt, just under the neckband, and perpendicular to the fold.

Use tailor's chalk to mark this line.
- Angle the ruler from the underarm seam to the horizontal line to shape the tunic. Again use chalk to mark this line Ⓐ.
- Pin the T-shirt and cut along these lines through all thicknesses. Unfold the shirt Ⓑ.

**2** Make the top/neckline casing:
- Fold under the top edge 1 inch (2.5 cm) and pin. Press on the fold with a hot iron, avoiding the pins. Repeat for the top back edge Ⓒ.
- On the front side, hand-sew a row of running stitches ¾ inches (1.9 cm) from the top folded edge with coordinating embroidery floss, catching the folded raw edge underneath Ⓓ. Repeat for the backside.

**3** Add the drawstring:
- Attach the safety pin to the end of the fold-over elastic and push it into the front channel, sliding the pin through until it comes out the other side Ⓔ. Pull about 12 inches (30.5 cm) through and slide the pin into the back channel on the backside Ⓕ, sliding the pin through until it comes out the other side.

- Try the tunic on and adjust the length of the elastic as needed. Tie the ends into a bow. Cut off excess elastic.

**4** Make cross-stitches with embroidery floss along the bottom edge of the T-shirt. Most shirts have two rows of top stitching at the bottom, which is a good guide for making the cross stitches at the top, bottom, or in between Ⓖ.

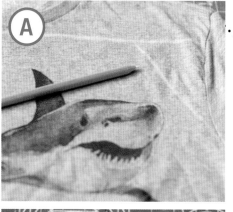

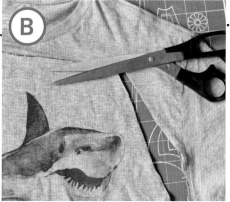

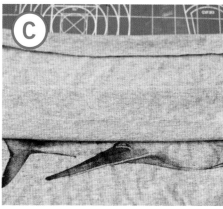

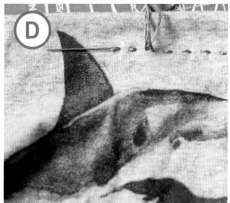

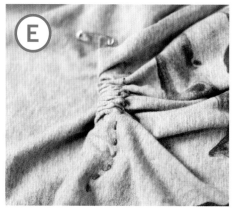

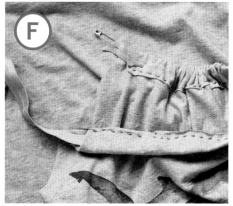

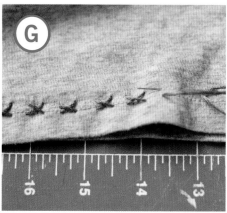

## nicole's Tips

- Jersey can be cut and it won't fray, so if the tunic is too long, measure how much you want to take off the bottom, chalk a line to guide you, and cut it off. No need to hem.

- T-shirts with armholes that are too big can be worn over a camisole for a layered look. They can also be taken in about an inch or so on the sides with a sewing machine to make them smaller. Shirts that are slimmer-fitting will have smaller armholes. Experimenting with different sizes and cuts will help you make the tunic that best fits your child's body.

- You can add stitches anywhere on the tunic, not just the bottom edge. Especially if you have an interesting graphic, you may want to outline words or a pattern with simple stitches.

# RIBBON OR T-REX TOTE

**Designer:** JENNY DOH

Boyish or girlie, choose the look you like best. These totes are easy to make with simple appliqués for loads of personality.

# Gather

### For each tote

- Basic Machine-Sewing Tool Kit (page 13)
- 2 pieces of cotton duck canvas fabric, 15 x 17 inches (38.1 x 43.2 cm)

### Ribbon Tote

- At least 7 different ribbons, each 16 inches (40.6 cm) long (the designer used by-the-spool ribbons by Offray)
- 1⅓ yards (1.2 m) of fuchsia cotton webbing, 1 inch (2.5 cm) wide

### T-Rex Tote

- T-Rex template (page 125)
- 1 piece of red felt, 10 x 8 inches (25.4 x 20.3 cm)
- Perle cotton (size 5), less than 1 skein of black
- 1⅓ yards (1.2 m) of black cotton webbing, 1 inch (2.5 cm) wide

### Finished Dimensions:

14 x 15 inches (35.6 x 38.1 cm)

### Seam allowance:

½ inch (1.3 mm)

# Make

## RIBBON TOTE FRONT

**1** Lay one of the cotton duck fabric pieces on a work surface with the short ends at the top and bottom.

**2** Use fabric spray adhesive to attach ribbons, starting 2 inches (5.1 cm) from the bottom edge. Allow the excess length of the ribbon to extend beyond both side edges Ⓐ (see page 97).

**3** Keep attaching ribbon, spaced approximately ½ inch (1.3 mm) apart, so that the top edge of the last ribbon is approximately 12 inches (30.5 cm) from the bottom edge of the fabric.

**4** Machine-stitch all the ribbons in place. For the wider ribbons, stitch along both long edges. For the thinner ribbons, stitch once along the center Ⓑ (see page 97).

**Option:** After assembling the tote, fold a piece of ribbon in half and pin the center to the front of the tote, approximately ½ inch (1.3 cm) from the top edge, centered in between the handle ends. Sew the center of the ribbon to the tote. Tie the ribbon into a bow.

## T-REX FRONT

**1** Use the template to trace the T-Rex shape onto the red felt and cut it out.

**2** Lay one of the cotton duck fabric pieces on a work surface with the short ends at the top and bottom. Use fabric spray adhesive to attach the cut felt, approximately 3 inches (7.6 cm) from the bottom edge.

**3** Hand-sew the felt onto the fabric with a running stitch, using black perle cotton. Make a French knot for the eye with the perle cotton. Make a running stitch with the perle cotton near the dinosaur's legs to create a horizon line Ⓒ.

## TO FINISH EITHER TOTE

**1** With wrong sides facing, fold the top edge of the fabric down 2 inches (5.2 cm) and press. Use pinking shears to trim the raw folded-down edge Ⓓ.

**2** Fold the cotton webbing in half and cut into two equal lengths. Position the raw ends of one strip onto the inner folded top edge, approximately 3½ inches (8.9 cm) from the sides and pin. Make sure the webbing isn't twisted.

**3** Machine-stitch along the entire top folded edge of the fabric, approximately ¼ inch (6 mm) down, securing the cotton webbing and removing pins as you go. Also stitch along the bottom edges of the webbing, approximately ¼ inch (6 mm) up.

**4** Repeat steps 1 through 3 for the backside of the tote.

**5** Pin the two sides together with the right sides facing. Stitch along one side, the bottom edge, and the remaining side of the tote. Use pinking shears to trim all sewn sides. Turn the tote right side out Ⓔ.

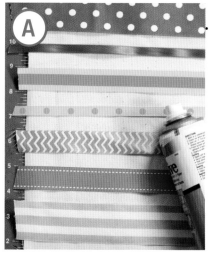

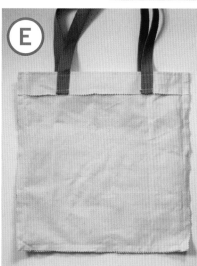

## jenny's Tips

- Ribbon Tote: Sew one or more ribbons to the back of the tote as well as the front, positioned vertically instead of horizontally.

- T-Rex Tote: Trace the template onto a stiff piece of paper (like a cereal box) and cut the image out with a sharp craft knife to make a stencil. Use the stencil and fabric paint to paint the image onto the tote.

# STARRY NIGHT STUFFED-ANIMAL SLEEPING BAGS

## Gather

- Basic Machine-Sewing Tool Kit (page 13)
- Starry Night template (page 115)
- ¼ yard (.2 m) quilting cotton, or 4 fat quarters of assorted cotton fabrics
- ¼ yard (.2 m) cotton batting
- Double-sided fusible interfacing
- 1 scrap of yellow quilting cotton
- Black embroidery floss
- Perle cotton (size 5), 1 skein of yellow
- Polyester fiberfill, less than 1 ounce

**Finished Dimensions:**

Small bag: 6 x 10 inches (15.2 x 25.4 cm)

Large bag: 8 x 12 inches (20.3 x 30.5 cm)

**Seam Allowance:**

¼ inch (6 mm)

**Designer:** MOLLIE JOHANSON

Bedtime can be extra special when your favorite stuffed animals get tucked in alongside you in their own cozy sleeping bags.

## Make

**1** Cut the following pieces:
Quilting cotton
- Small bag: Cut 2 pieces, 6½ x 17 inches (16.5 x 43.2 cm)
- Large bag: Cut 2 pieces, 8½ x 22 inches (21.6 x 55.9 cm)

Cotton batting
- Small bag: Cut 1 piece, 6½ x 17 inches (16.5 x 43.2 cm)
- Large bag: Cut 1 piece, 8½ x 22 inches (21.6 x 55.9 cm)

Fusible interfacing
- Cut 1 piece for each bag, 2½ x 7 inches (6.4 x 17.8 cm)

**2** Make the bag body:
- With right sides facing, stack the two quilting cotton pieces for the small bag. Pin these layers on top of the corresponding piece of batting.

- Machine-stitch around all edges, leaving a 3-inch (7.6 cm) opening on one of the short sides. Clip the corners to reduce bulk then turn the sleeping bag right side out Ⓐ (see next page).
- Repeat to make the large bag.

**3** With a pencil, trace the star template onto the paper side of the fusible interfacing six times. Following manufacturer's instructions, iron the non-paper side onto the wrong side of the yellow quilting cotton and cut out the stars Ⓑ (see next page).

**4** Peel the paper backing off of two of the stars and embroider a face with three strands of black embroidery floss. Make French knots for the eyes and back stitches for the mouth Ⓑ (see next page).

**5** Fold over the short end of each sleeping bag, stopping about 3 inches (7.6 cm) below the open short end of the bag. For each bag, position the two plain stars and one embroidered star on the folded top side of the bag. Fuse in place with an iron. Unfold the bag and stitch along the edges of all the stars with a running stitch, using perle cotton Ⓒ.

**6** About 3 inches (7.6 cm) from the open end of the sleeping bag, hand-sew a line of running stitches across the width of the bag, using the perle cotton. This will section off the pillow Ⓓ.

**7** Push fiberfill stuffing into the openings to form the pillow. Sew the openings closed Ⓔ.

**8** Fold the front of each sleeping bag up to the line of the running stitch and pin in place. Stitch the sides closed with a herringbone stitch, using the perle cotton Ⓕ.

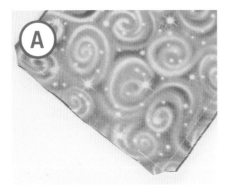

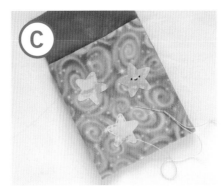

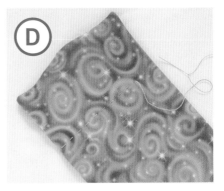

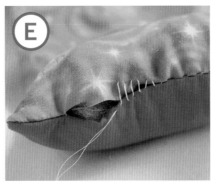

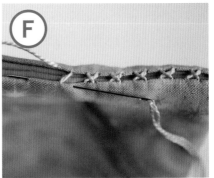

## *mollie's* Tips

- Stitching through the layers of fabric and batting with perle cotton can be tricky, so be sure to use a large enough needle for less frustration.

- Instead of adding stars, sew on an embroidered patch with the name of your favorite stuffed friend!

# SUPERHERO CAPE AND MASK

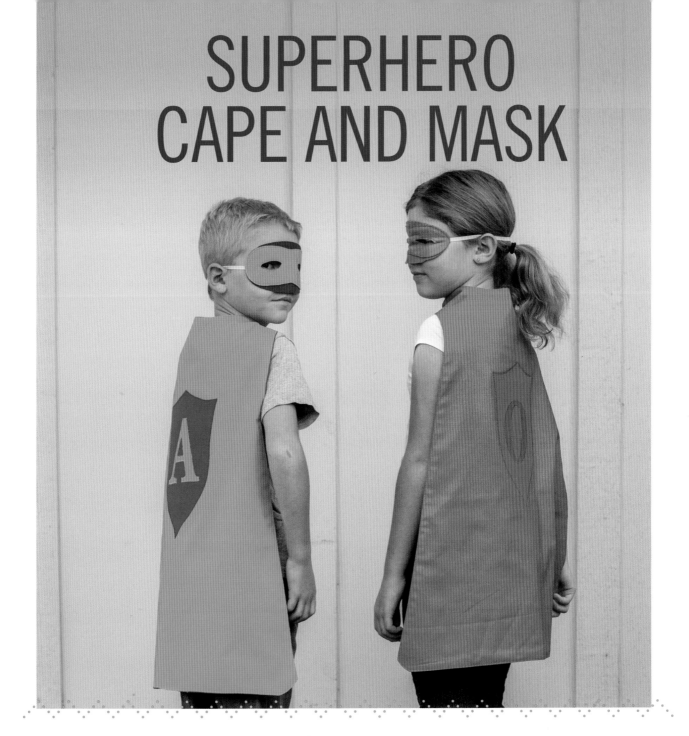

**Designer:** HEATHER JONES

These instructions are for the orange and blue cape.
If you have a second superhero in your life, make
another set with a different color combination.

# Gather

- Basic Machine-Sewing Tool Kit (page 13)
- Shield and mask templates (pages 119)
- 1 yard (.9 m) of orange cotton fabric, 42-inch (106.7 cm) wide
- 1 yard (.9 m) of blue cotton fabric, 42-inch (106.7 cm) wide
- Yardstick
- Bowl or plate with 8-inch (20.3 cm) diameter
- ½ yard (.5 m) of paper-backed fusible webbing
- Computer and printer
- White copy paper

- Craft felt sheets in orange and blue
- Thread to coordinate with both felt colors
- 1 inch (2.5 cm) of Velcro, ⅝ inches (1.6 cm) wide
- 12 inches (30.5 cm) of braided elastic, ¼ inch (6 mm) wide

**Finished Dimensions:**

Cape: 22 x 29 inches (55.9 x 73.7 cm)
Mask: 6¼ x 3¼ inches (15.9 x 8.3 cm)

**Seam Allowance:**

¼ inch (6 mm)

# Make

## THE CAPE

**1** Cut the fabric. Use a rotary cutter, quilting ruler, and cutting mat to cut the orange and blue fabrics into pieces that measure 30 inches x WOF (76.2 cm x width of fabric). Set the remaining fabric portions aside to use in step 4.

**2** With the illustration (page 105) as reference, draft the cape shape.
- Fold the cut orange fabric with the two long sides aligned and press.
- Lay the folded fabric on a table with the long folded edge at the left side.

- With a water-soluble marker, mark 6 inches (15.2 cm) to the right of the fold, on the top side, and 12 inches (30.5 cm) to the right of the fold on the bottom side. Use a yardstick to draw a line to connect the two marks.
- Place the bowl or plate on the narrow edge of the cape, about 5 inches (12.7 cm) from the top edge, and 3½ inches (8.9 cm) to the right of the fold. Trace the curve with the water-soluble marker.

**3** Cut out the cape shapes.
- Cut out the orange cape along the marked lines.
- The cape has two corners on each shoulder strap and two corners at the hem edges. Use the water-soluble marker to draw rounded corners on all of these, and trim with scissors.
- Lay the blue fabric out flat. Using the orange fabric as a template, trace around it onto the blue fabric. Cut along the traced lines with scissors.

**4** Prepare the shield appliqué
- Cut a piece from remaining blue fabric that measures 8½ x 10½ inches (21.6 x 26.7 cm), and cut a piece of fusible webbing the same size.
- Cut a piece from the remaining orange fabric that measures 8 inches (20.3 cm) square and cut a piece of fusible webbing 7½ inches (19 cm) square. Set these aside.

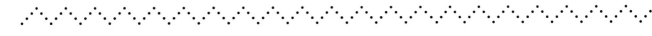

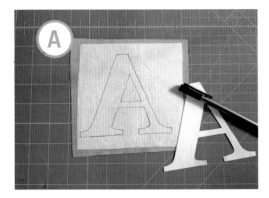

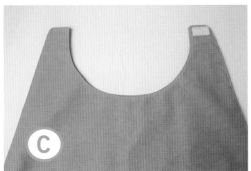

- Trace the shield template on a piece of paper and cut it out with a pair of scissors. Set aside.
- Use word-processing computer software to create a pattern for the letter of your choice. (I used a capital letter in the font Georgia, set to bold and to the size of 400 point, but feel free to make it in another font or size if you prefer.) Once you have created the letter that you like, print out the document on plain white copy paper. Cut out the letter carefully with scissors Ⓐ.
- Following manufacturer's directions, adhere the non-paper side of the large fusible webbing to the wrong side of the blue fabric. Center and fuse the smaller webbing to the orange fabric.

5 Apply the shield to the cape.
- Trace the shield pattern piece on the paper side of the fused blue fabric and cut it out.
- Trace the initial pattern in reverse (flip it left to right) on the paper side of the fused orange fabric and cut it out.
- Lay the orange cape flat and measure down from the center fold at the neckline 5 inches (12.7 cm). Mark the

spot with a pin. Remove the paper backing of the shield appliqué and center it on the cape's fold line with the top point at the pin mark. Following the manufacturer's directions, fuse it in place with a hot iron.
- Remove the paper backing of the orange letter appliqué and fuse in place with a hot iron Ⓑ.
- Machine-stitch around the perimeter of each appliqué piece with a tight zigzag stitch and coordinating thread.

6 Construct the cape as follows.
- With right sides facing, pin the orange and blue cape pieces together. Starting at the bottom center, backstitch and then sew along the entire perimeter, leaving a 4-inch (10.2 cm) opening, on the bottom edge, backstitching again at the end.
- Use scissors to snip the seam allowances of the curved areas of the cape, making sure to not snip the seamline threads. This will allow the curved areas to lay flat.
- Turn the cape right side out through the 4-inch (10.2 cm) opening and press.

SUPERHERO CAPE AND MASK **103**

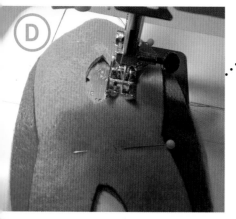

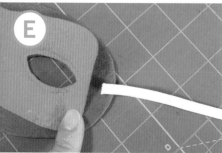

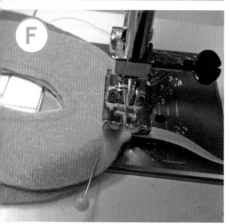

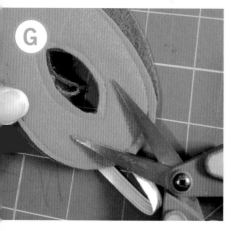

- Turn the seam allowances of the opening to the inside of the cape and pin in place. Top stitch along the perimeter of the cape with coordinating thread and backstitch to lock the stitches in place.

**7** Add Velcro tabs. Cut a pair of 1-inch (2.5 cm) long Velcro squares. Sew one piece to the top of the collar strap on the right side and sew the other piece to the bottom of the collar strap on the left side Ⓒ (see page 103).

## THE MASK

**1** Use Template B (outer mask) to trace and cut one piece from the blue felt. Use Template C (inner mask) to trace and cut one piece from the orange felt.

**2** Place the orange felt piece on top of the blue felt piece and topstitch around each of the eye openings with coordinating thread Ⓓ. Remove the mask from the sewing machine.

**3** Pin ½ inch (6 mm) of one end of the elastic between the two felt pieces, near one of the eyes. Place the other end of the elastic between the felt pieces on the opposite side, making sure to keep the elastic untwisted Ⓔ.

**4** Top stitch along the perimeter of the orange felt with coordinating thread, making sure to catch the elastic while you sew Ⓕ. Backstitch to lock the seam and snip threads with a pair of scissors Ⓖ.

## heather's Tips

- To save ink during printing, select the outline mode for the letter before printing.
- For a different look (and less fusing and sewing), make a stencil of the letter with an empty cereal box and use the stencil to paint the letter on the shield with fabric paint.

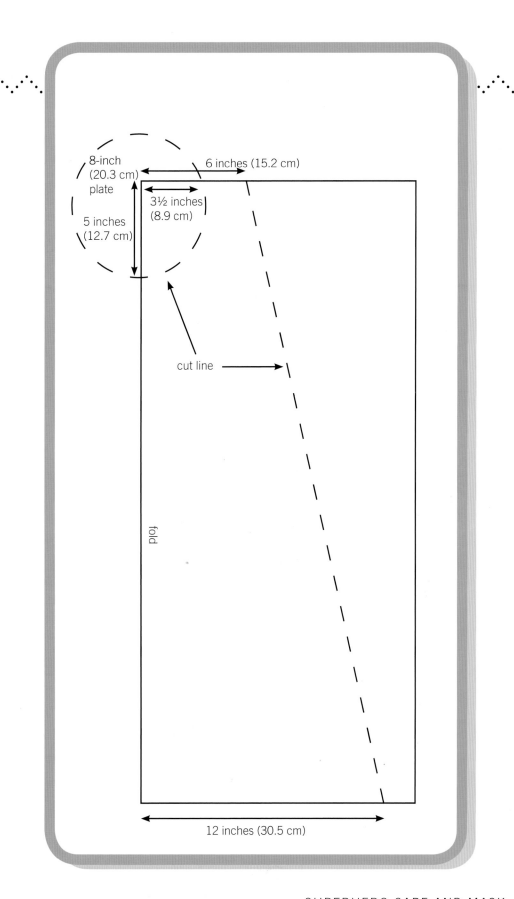

8-inch (20.3 cm) plate

6 inches (15.2 cm)

3½ inches (8.9 cm)

5 inches (12.7 cm)

cut line

fold

12 inches (30.5 cm)

# WOOLY BOMBER CAP

**Designer:** NICOLE BLUM

Use the small templates for a baby or wee toddler and the larger templates for any other-sized kid. Even a woman with an average-sized head can wear this cap!

# Gather

- Basic Hand-Sewing Tool Kit (page 9)
- Felted wool or cashmere sweater
- Bomber Cap Templates (page 123)*
- 6-strand embroidery floss: 1 skein in light blue (or other color to coordinate with your felted sweater)

*Templates provided are for a baby size and a child/woman size. The directions shown here are for the child/woman size.*

## felting tip

To felt a wool sweater, wash it in hot water and then dry it in high heat. Washing the sweater with other items, such as denim jeans, will help the felting process as the wool agitates with the other garments.

# Make

**1** Cut out the pieces.

- Lay the felted sweater flat on a work surface.
- Place both enlarged templates on top of the sweater. It is important that they are aligned top to bottom, so the stretch on the sweater is running the right way. *Note:* You can use a sweater that has holes as long as you avoid them.
- Carefully trace around the templates with tailor's chalk Ⓐ.
- Pin the sweater layers together inside the shapes and cut them out Ⓑ. You will have two of each. Note where the front of each side panel is (the gently curved edge marked on the template), so they are both oriented the right way when sewing the pieces together. Also note which is the right side of the sweater; if you find it hard to tell, make a little chalk mark on the right side.

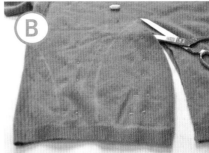

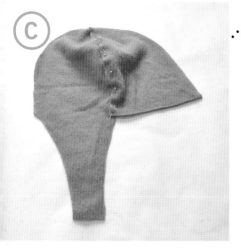

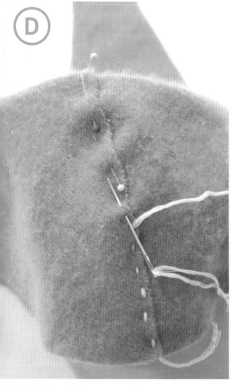

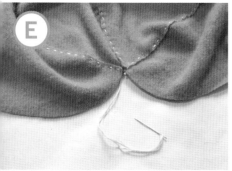

**2** Assemble the front sides; decide which of the front/back pieces will be the front then do the following:

- Overlap the left side of the front panel to the front side of one of the side panel pieces and pin Ⓒ.
- Starting from the top point of the overlap (the crown of the hat), sew a small running stitch along the overlap with the embroidery floss, about ¼ inch (6mm) from the raw edge, making sure that you go through both layers of wool, and removing pins as you go Ⓓ.
- Make your last stich approximately 1 inch (2.5 cm) from the end and tie a knot on the right side to secure.
- Overlap the other side of the front panel piece to the front side of the second side panel. Pin and sew together with a running stitch.

**3** Attach the back:

- Repeat step 2 to attach the back panel to the backsides of the two side panels with a running stitch Ⓔ. *Note: When sewing on the back panel, you may have a tricky time getting both sides to end in just the right spot. Not to worry. Once they are sewn in place, use a ruler to draw a straight line with chalk from one corner to the other (where the side panels have those pointy parts) and simply cut so that it is even.*

**4** Finish the hat:

- Turn up the 1 inch (1.5 cm) of wool from the front panel that has not been stitched to the side panels and pin Ⓕ.
- Use embroidery floss to make small cross stitches through both thicknesses Ⓖ.
- Optional: Add a large cross stich at the top of the hat. It's a cute accent that adds some reinforcement to keep everything together Ⓗ.

(F)

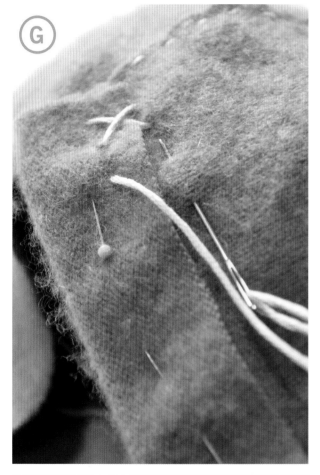

(G)

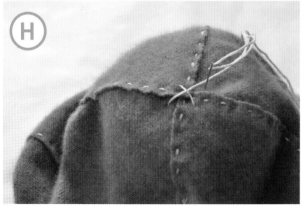

(H)

## nicole's Tips

- It's important to try to make hand stitches small and close together. Big stitches that run quickly down the seam will show gaps and won't make a strong garment. Take your time and be proud of your strong sewing!

- You can add decorations on the earflaps and anywhere on the hat. You could also make a tassel from yarn to hang off the top.

# TEMPLATES

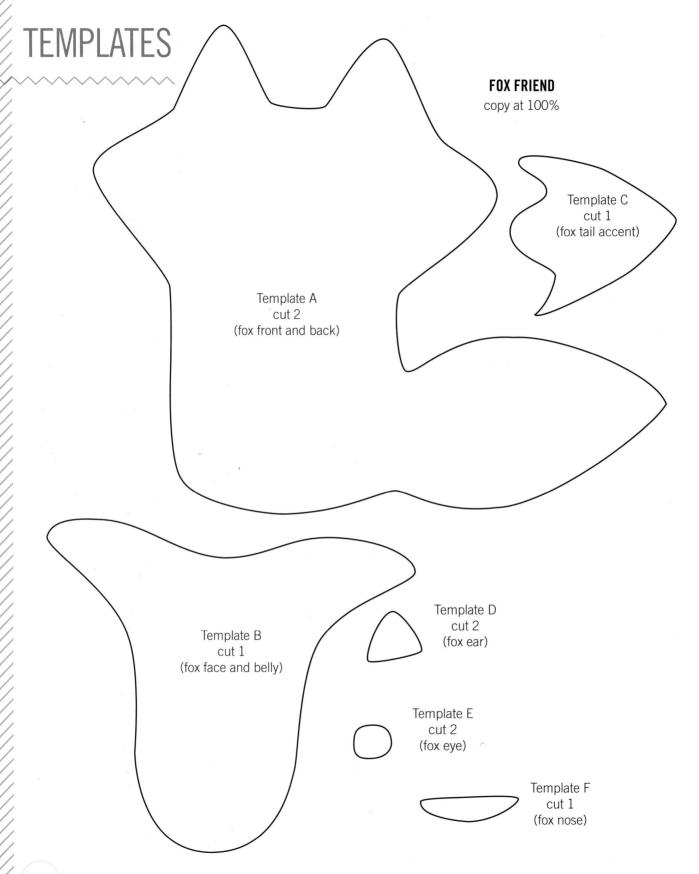

**FOX FRIEND**
copy at 100%

Template C
cut 1
(fox tail accent)

Template A
cut 2
(fox front and back)

Template B
cut 1
(fox face and belly)

Template D
cut 2
(fox ear)

Template E
cut 2
(fox eye)

Template F
cut 1
(fox nose)

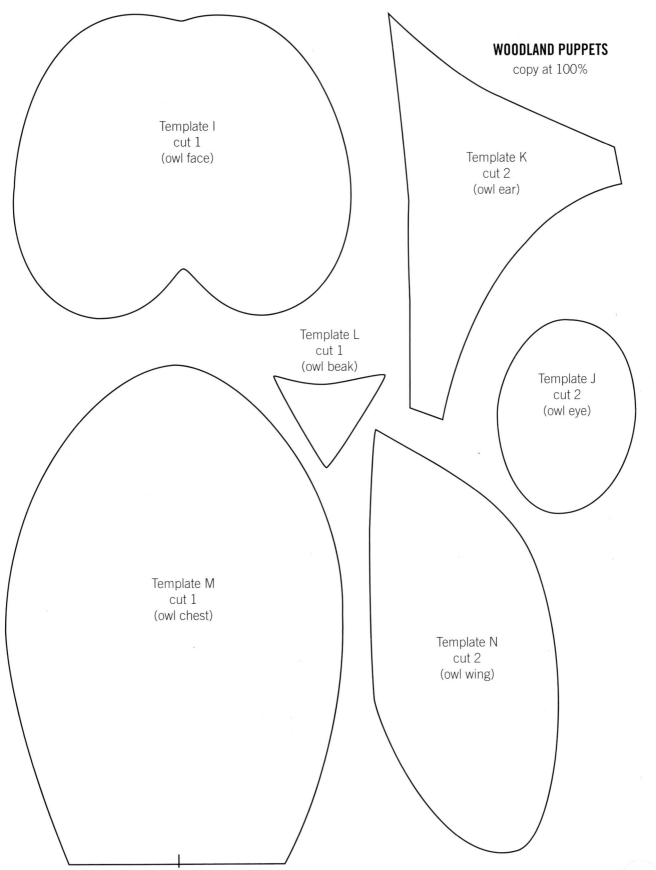

Template I
cut 1
(owl face)

Template K
cut 2
(owl ear)

**WOODLAND PUPPETS**
copy at 100%

Template L
cut 1
(owl beak)

Template J
cut 2
(owl eye)

Template M
cut 1
(owl chest)

Template N
cut 2
(owl wing)

# TEMPLATES

**WOODLAND PUPPETS**
copy at 100%

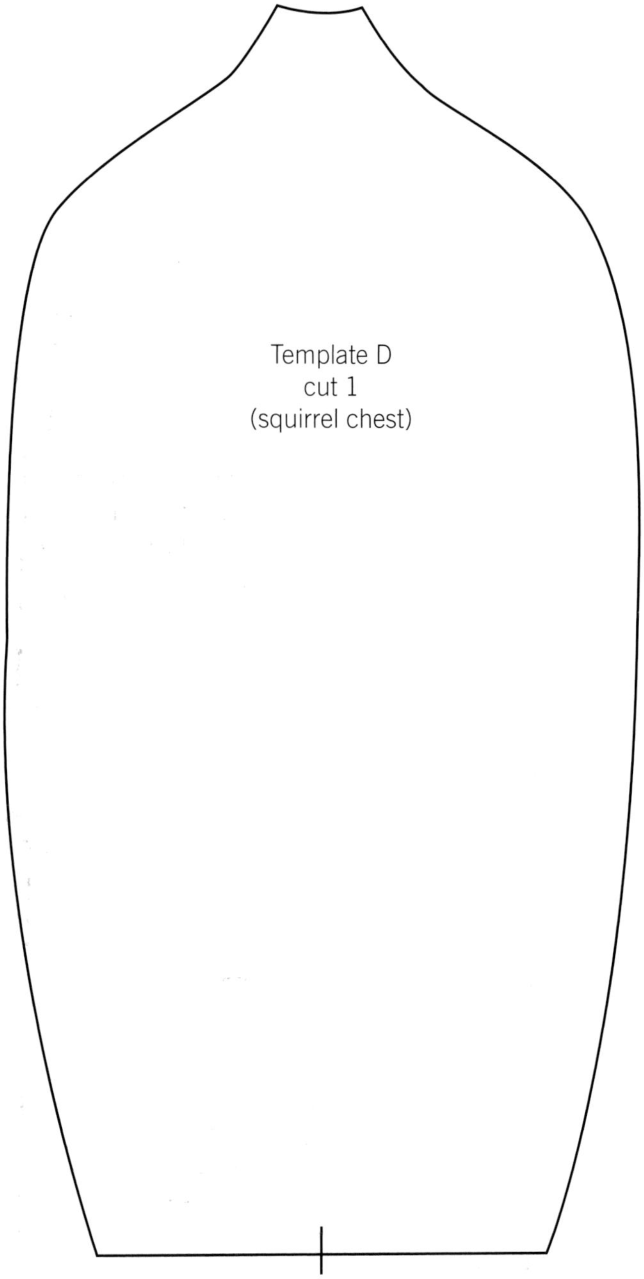

Template E
cut 1
(squirrel tail)

Template D
cut 1
(squirrel chest)

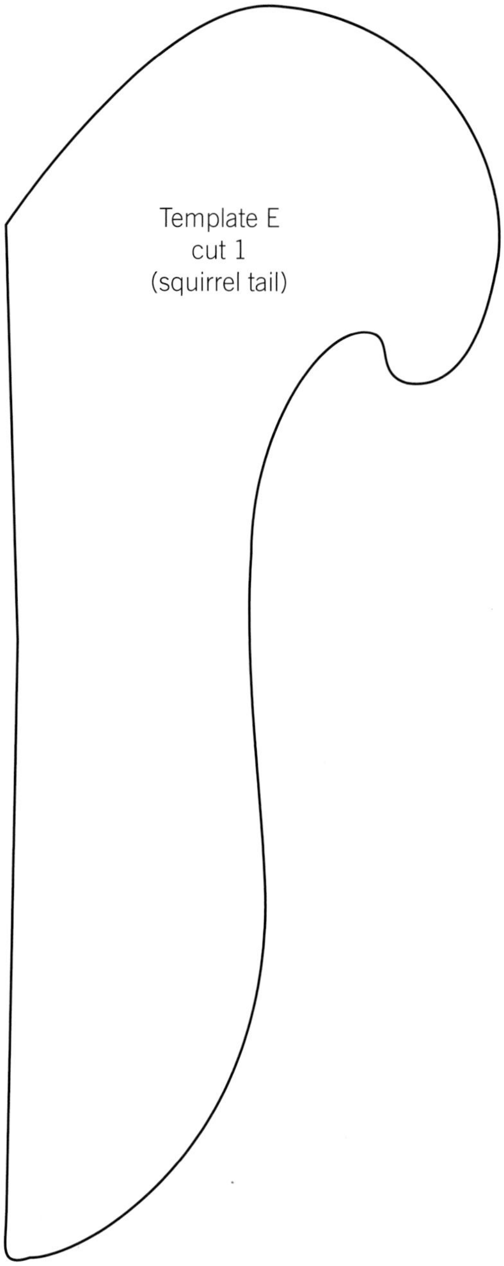

Template F
cut 1
(squirrel nose)

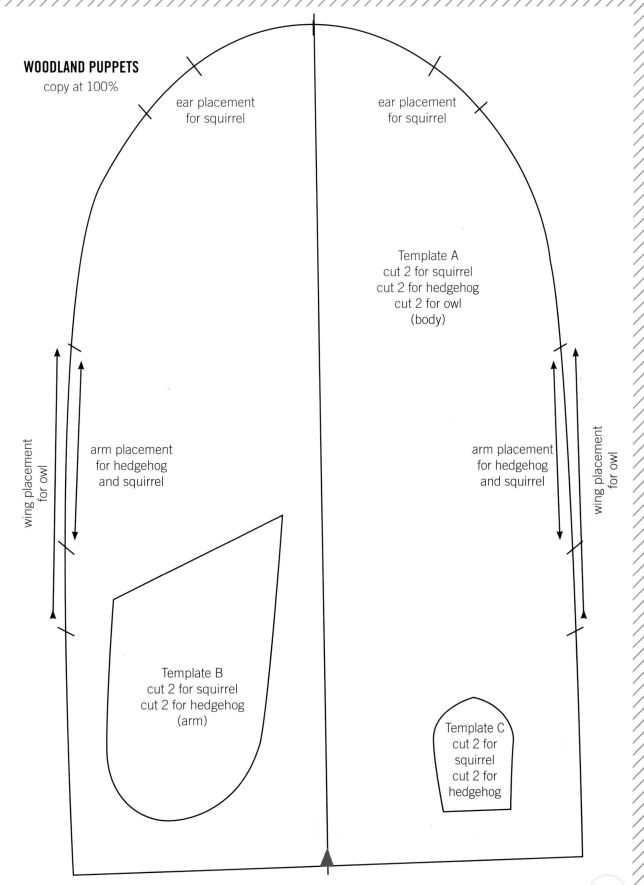

**WOODLAND PUPPETS**
copy at 100%

ear placement
for squirrel

ear placement
for squirrel

Template A
cut 2 for squirrel
cut 2 for hedgehog
cut 2 for owl
(body)

wing placement
for owl

arm placement
for hedgehog
and squirrel

arm placement
for hedgehog
and squirrel

wing placement
for owl

Template B
cut 2 for squirrel
cut 2 for hedgehog
(arm)

Template C
cut 2 for
squirrel
cut 2 for
hedgehog

# TEMPLATES

**WOODLAND PUPPETS**
copy at 100%

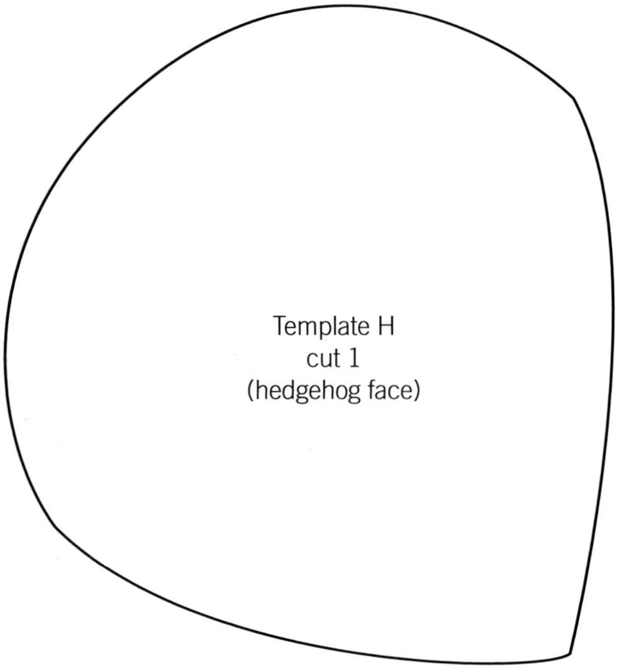
Template H
cut 1
(hedgehog face)

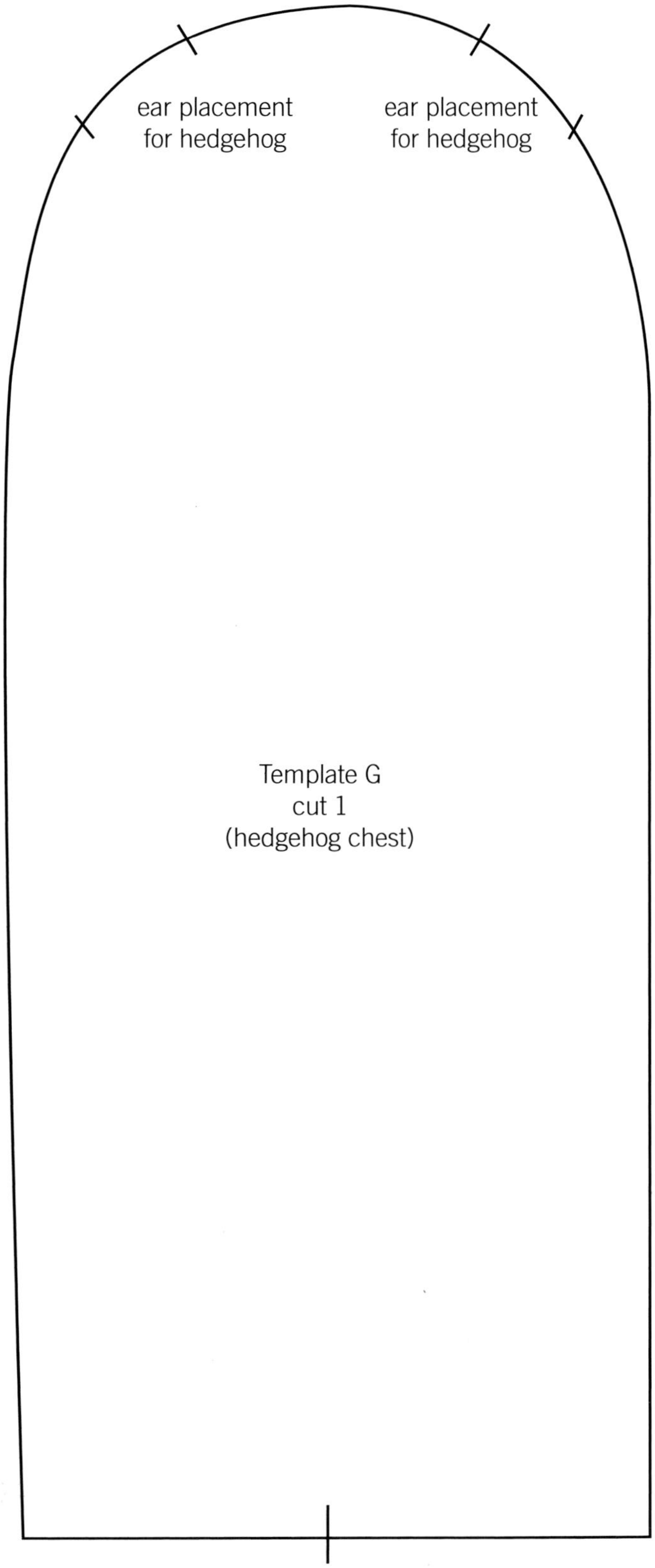
ear placement
for hedgehog
ear placement
for hedgehog
Template G
cut 1
(hedgehog chest)

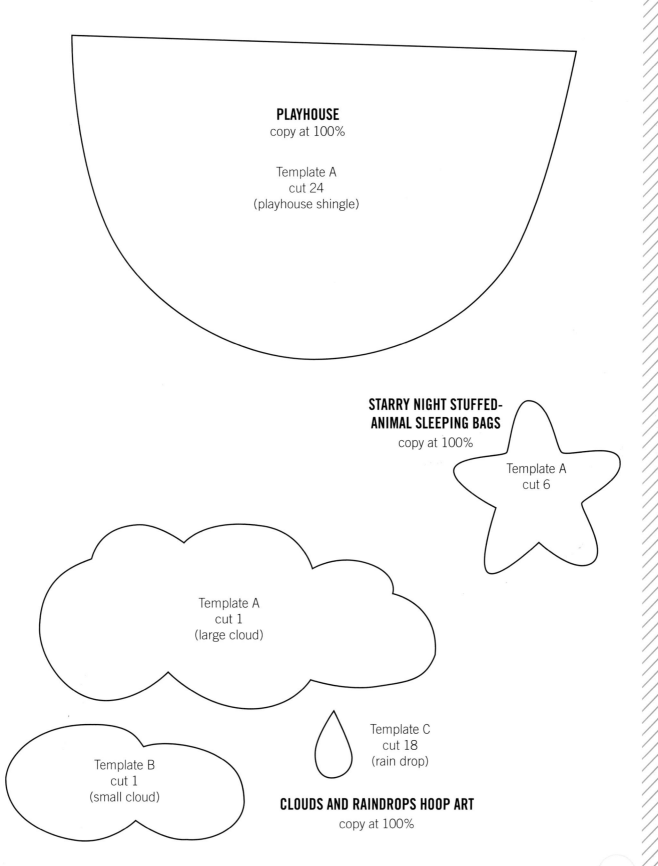

**PLAYHOUSE**
copy at 100%

Template A
cut 24
(playhouse shingle)

**STARRY NIGHT STUFFED-
ANIMAL SLEEPING BAGS**
copy at 100%

Template A
cut 6

Template A
cut 1
(large cloud)

Template C
cut 18
(rain drop)

Template B
cut 1
(small cloud)

**CLOUDS AND RAINDROPS HOOP ART**
copy at 100%

**SEWN PAPER
CANDY POUCHES**
enlarge 200%

Template A
cut 2
(alien front/back)

**ALIEN STAND-UP DOLLS**
enlarge 200%

Template B
cut 3
(alien base)

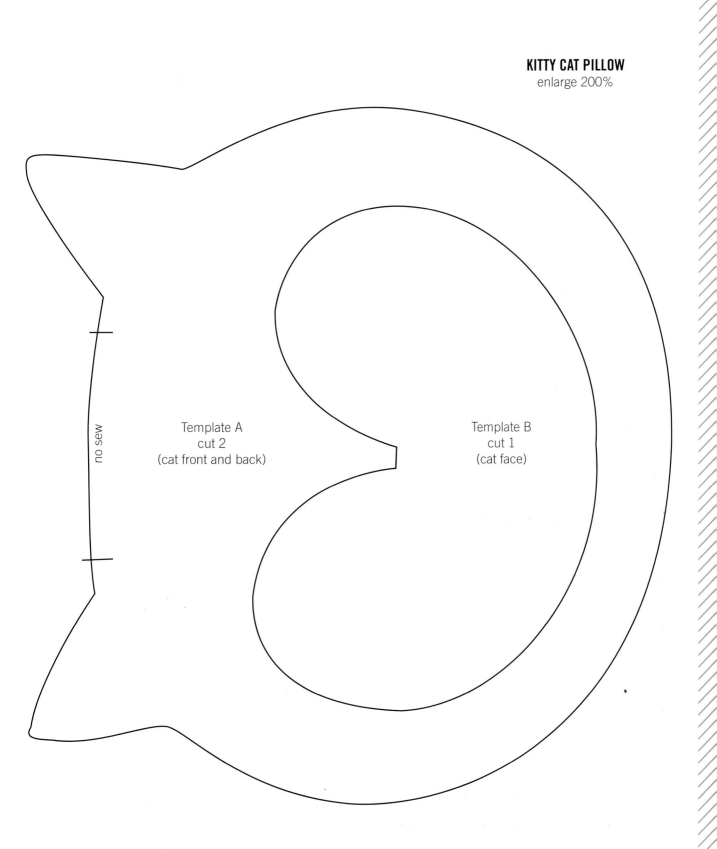

**KITTY CAT PILLOW**
enlarge 200%

no sew

Template A
cut 2
(cat front and back)

Template B
cut 1
(cat face)

# TEMPLATES

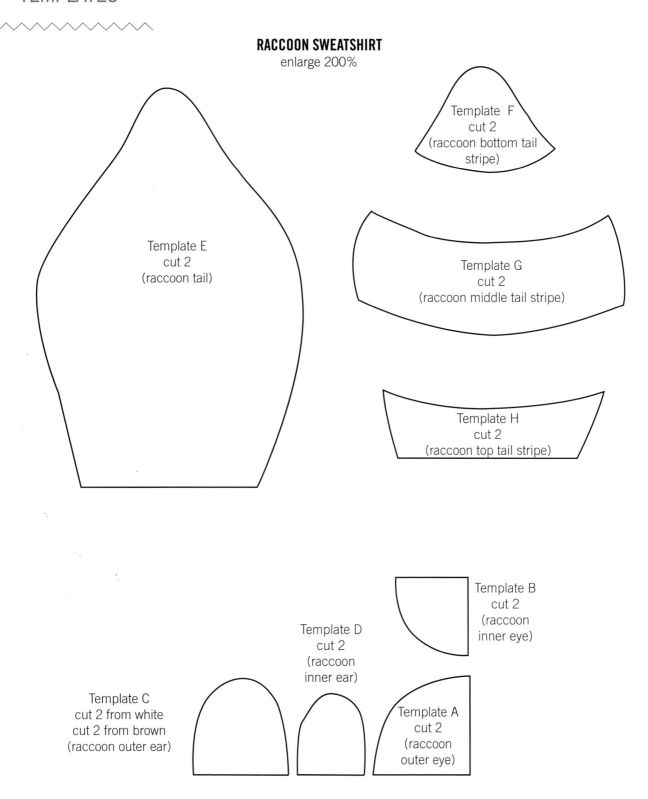

**RACCOON SWEATSHIRT**
enlarge 200%

Template E
cut 2
(raccoon tail)

Template F
cut 2
(raccoon bottom tail
stripe)

Template G
cut 2
(raccoon middle tail stripe)

Template H
cut 2
(raccoon top tail stripe)

Template B
cut 2
(raccoon
inner eye)

Template D
cut 2
(raccoon
inner ear)

Template C
cut 2 from white
cut 2 from brown
(raccoon outer ear)

Template A
cut 2
(raccoon
outer eye)

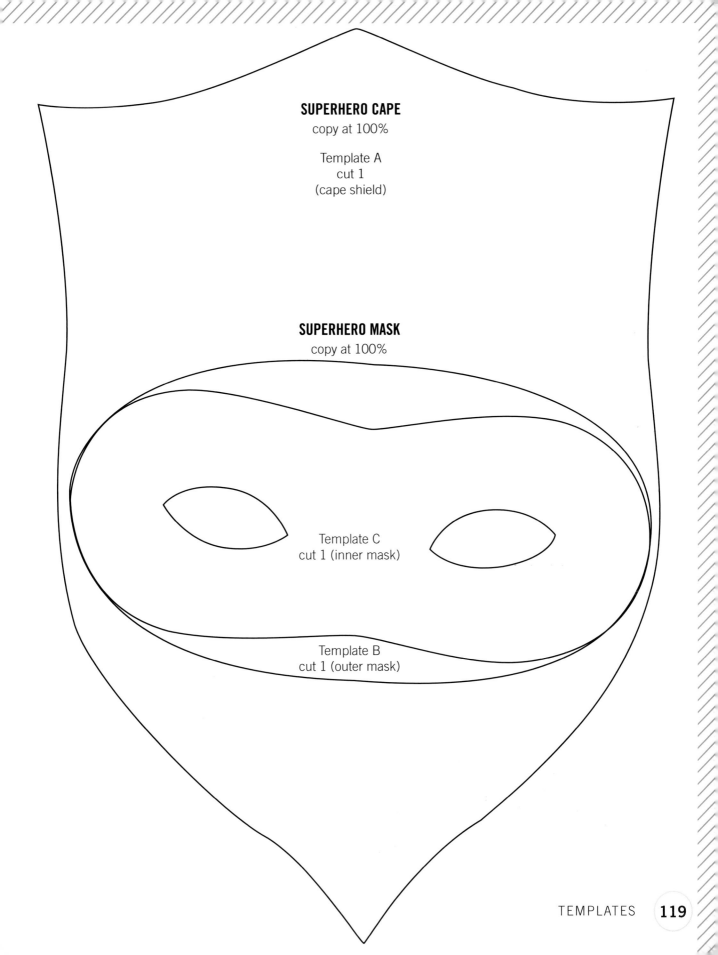

**SUPERHERO CAPE**

copy at 100%

Template A
cut 1
(cape shield)

**SUPERHERO MASK**

copy at 100%

Template C
cut 1 (inner mask)

Template B
cut 1 (outer mask)

**ANIMAL HEADBANDS**
enlarge 200%

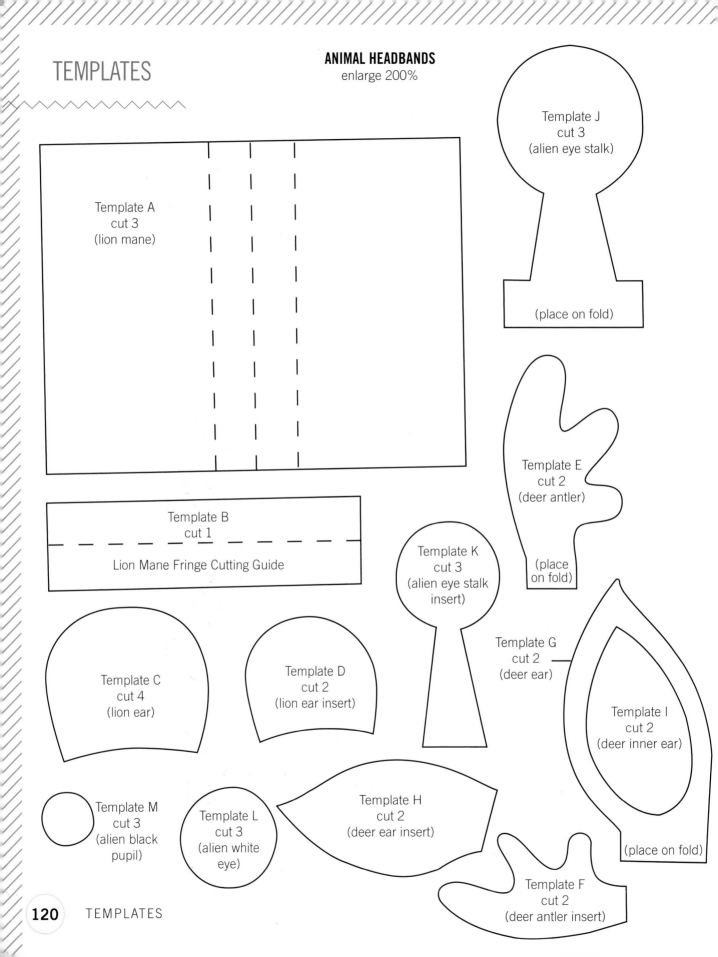

Template J
cut 3
(alien eye stalk)

(place on fold)

Template A
cut 3
(lion mane)

Template E
cut 2
(deer antler)

(place
on fold)

Template B
cut 1

Lion Mane Fringe Cutting Guide

Template K
cut 3
(alien eye stalk
insert)

Template G
cut 2
(deer ear)

Template C
cut 4
(lion ear)

Template D
cut 2
(lion ear insert)

Template I
cut 2
(deer inner ear)

Template M
cut 3
(alien black
pupil)

Template L
cut 3
(alien white
eye)

Template H
cut 2
(deer ear insert)

(place on fold)

Template F
cut 2
(deer antler insert)

**MONOGRAM PILLOW**
enlarge 400%

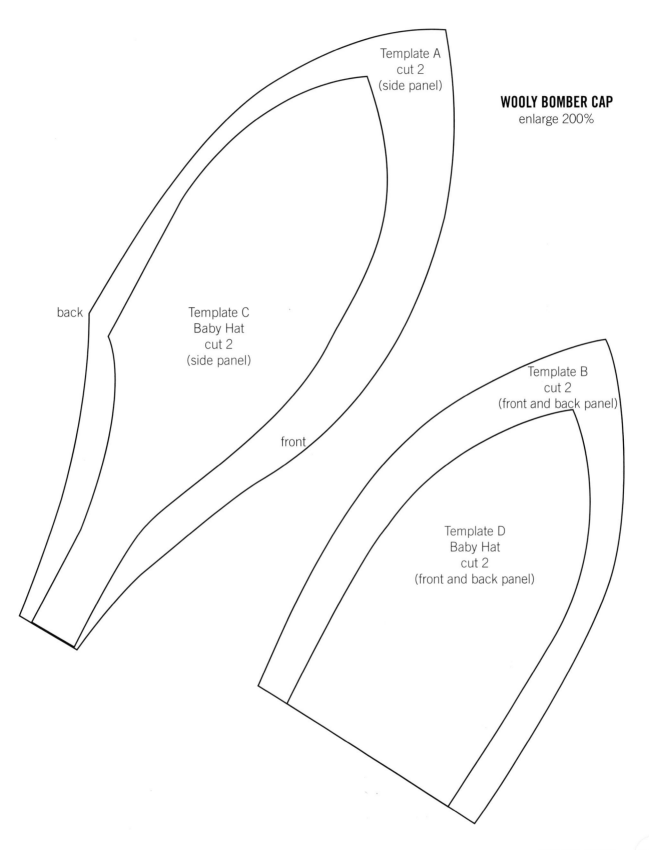

Template A
cut 2
(side panel)

**WOOLY BOMBER CAP**
enlarge 200%

back

Template C
Baby Hat
cut 2
(side panel)

front

Template B
cut 2
(front and back panel)

Template D
Baby Hat
cut 2
(front and back panel)

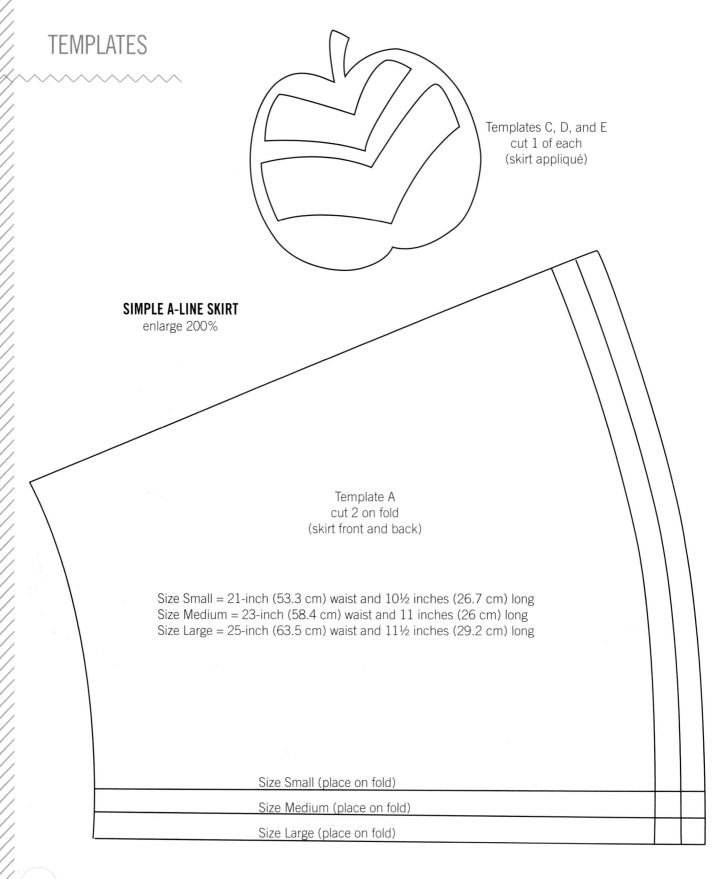

Templates C, D, and E
cut 1 of each
(skirt appliqué)

### SIMPLE A-LINE SKIRT
enlarge 200%

Template A
cut 2 on fold
(skirt front and back)

Size Small = 21-inch (53.3 cm) waist and 10½ inches (26.7 cm) long
Size Medium = 23-inch (58.4 cm) waist and 11 inches (26 cm) long
Size Large = 25-inch (63.5 cm) waist and 11½ inches (29.2 cm) long

Size Small (place on fold)

Size Medium (place on fold)

Size Large (place on fold)

**SIMPLE A-LINE SKIRT**
enlarge 200%

Template B
cut 1 on fold
(skirt waistband)

**T-REX TOTE**
copy at 100%

Size Small
(place on fold)

Size Medium
(place on fold)

Size Large
(place on fold)

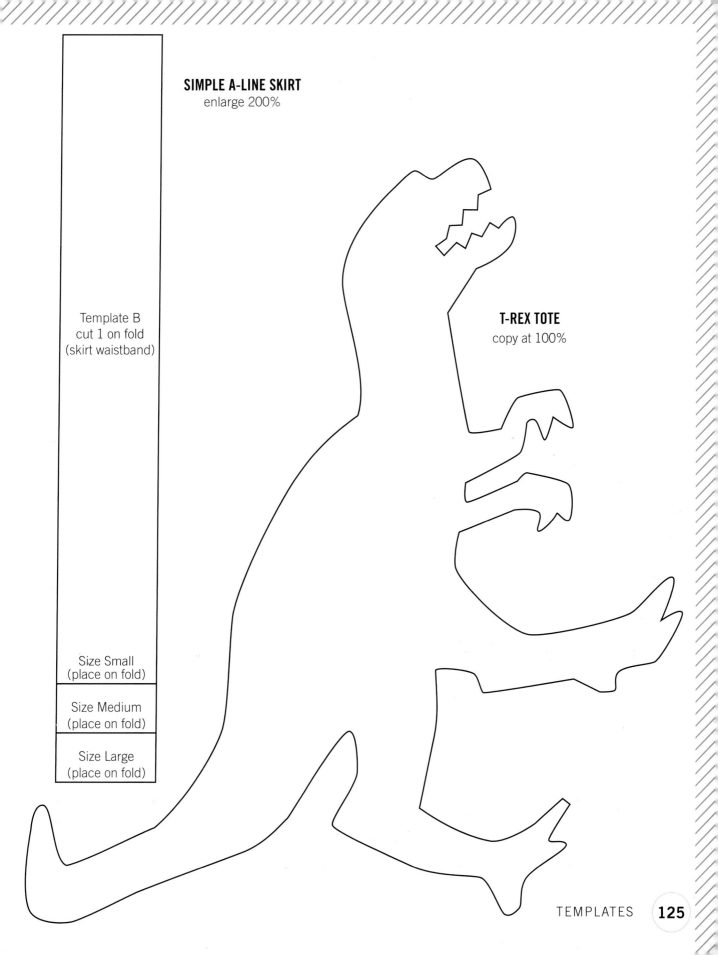

# ABOUT THE CONTRIBUTORS

**NICOLE BLUM** is a freelance crafter and stylist for *Family Fun* magazine, author of *Improv Sewing*. She and her husband live in rural western Massachusetts and are founders of Carr's Ciderhouse where they press apples from their orchard and handcraft artisanal hard ciders. To learn more, visit *www.improvdiary.com*.

**JENNY DOH** is in love with making art. She has authored and packaged numerous books and runs an art studio where she teaches painting. She also hosts visiting artists who teach methods in arts and crafts. She lives in Santa Ana, California. To learn more, visit *www.crescendoh.com*.

**JAMEY EKINS** lives with her family in beautiful Victoria, British Columbia where she works as a graphic designer by day and a creative adventurer of assorted arts and crafts at all other times of the day. To learn more, visit *www.dabblesandbabbles.com*.

**CHERI HEATON** is a creative mother of three children. She is author of the blog, I Am Momma Hear Me Roar. She writes about sewing, decorating, and motherhood. She and her work have been featured in various magazines and on television, including an appearance on *The Martha Stewart Show*. Cherie always has an idea in her head and a project in-progress in her garage. Visit *www.iammommahearmeroar.net*.

**JOEL HENRIQUES** has devoted himself to making arts and crafts both accessible and meaningful. Through his projects, Joel encourages everyone, regardless of economic means, skill level, or age, to participate in the collective creative process. Learn more at *www.madebyjoel.com*.

**LAURA HOWARD** is a designer, maker, blogger, and craft writer who lives near London, England. She is author of two books: *Super-Cute Felt* and *Super-Cute Felt Animals*. In her spare time, she likes to knit, bake, embroider, and craft with paper. Learn more at *www.bugsandfishes.blogspot.com*.

**MEGAN HUNT** is the voice behind the popular lifestyle and creative blog, Princess Lasertron, as well as a wedding designer and maker of custom flower bouquets and dresses. Megan speaks at creative and entrepreneurial conferences around the country. She recently co-founded Hello Holiday, an online fashion startup that offers support and funding to new designers. She lives in Omaha, Nebraska with her daughter, Alice. To learn more, visit *www.princesslasertron.com*.

**MOLLIE JOHANSON** was trained as a graphic designer but spends most of her time working on embroidery, sewing, and other small craft projects for her blog, shop, and assorted books and magazines. Her work is identified by sweet smiling faces that she adds to just about everything. Mollie lives with her family in Chicago. To learn more, visit *www.molliejohanson.com*.

**HEATHER JONES** is a designer and self-taught quilter who lives outside Cincinnati, Ohio with her husband and children. She is inspired by everyday places and objects and is always excited by the challenge to translate that inspiration into her work. Heather has a great love and respect for the traditional art of quilting, is an avid collector of vintage quilts, and loves to bring a modern twist to traditional patterns. To learn more, visit *www.oliveandollie.com*.

**CAL PATCH** has been a maker since she was a Girl Scout in the 1970s. She sews, crochets, drafts sewing patterns, spins, embroiders, knits, prints, and dyes. Hence the name of her clothing label: hodge podge. Cal has taught fiber arts for more than a decade at shops and retreats around the country. After 17 years of being a New York City dweller, Cal recently relocated to the rural Catskills where she is learning to be a crafty farmer. She is author of *Design-It-Yourself Clothes: Patternmaking Simplified.* To learn more, visit *www.hodgepodgefarm.net.*

**SUSAN PHILLIPS** lives with her family in sunny California. With a knack for creating since she was young, Susan enjoys spreading inspiration with unique designs on her blog and as a freelance writer for various DIY websites and sewing magazines. While specializing in home décor and children's clothing, she is devoted to keeping her designs fresh and modern. To learn more, visit *www.livingwithpunks.com.*

**MARY RASCH** resides with her husband, daughter, and son in northern Minnesota near the shore of Lake Superior. She is passionate about the creative process, and loves to sew, knit, paint, draw, and take photos. Her work has been featured in numerous books and magazines. To learn more, visit *www.maryrasch.com.*

**AIMEE RAY** is an indie business owner with a passion for crafting, nature, and sci-fi. She is author of the *Doodle Stitching* series of books on creative embroidery. A midwestern Illinois girl at heart, Aimee currently resides in Arkansas with her husband, Josh, and their two dogs. To learn more about her, visit *www.dreamfollow.com.*

**CYNTHIA SHAFFER** is a mixed media artist, quilter, and creative sewer. She is the author of *Stash Happy Patchwork, Stash Happy Appliqué*, and co-author of *Serge It!.* Cynthia lives in Orange, California. To learn more, visit *www.cynthiashaffer.com.*

**KATHLEEN WALCK** lives in Pennsylvania Dutch Country and is inspired by the traditional arts and crafts in the region. Prior to motherhood, Kathleen worked as an art teacher, museum educator, and artist. She currently strives to live creatively every day, through knitting, cooking, crafting, or by simply playing with her two young sons.

**ANNABEL WRIGLEY** is a sewing teacher and author. She owns Little Pincushion Studio, a bright little sewing studio for children in the countryside of Virginia. She teaches many creative kids everything they need in order to become independent sewists. To learn more, visit *www.littlepincushionstudio.com.*

**Editors:** CONNIE SANTISTEBAN and BETH SWEET

**Technical Copyeditor:** NANCY D. WOOD

**Assistant Editors:** AMANDA CRABTREE WESTON and MONICA MOUET

**Designer:** RAQUEL JOYA

**Photographer:** CYNTHIA SHAFFER

**Models:** GWENDOLYN ALVARADO, SARAH CHIASSON, PAIGE DEFRANCISCO, ELLA FURRY, OLIVIA FURRY, FLYNN STAAB, MARISOL STAAB, JENNIFER TAYLOR, AMANDA VENTO, and JUSTIN VENTO

# INDEX

# ABOUT THE AUTHOR

Jenny Doh has authored and packaged numerous books including *Washi Wonderful*, *Crochet Love*, *Craft-a-Doodle*, *Print Collective*, *Creative Lettering*, *Stamp It!*, *Journal It!*, and *We Make Dolls!*. She lives in Santa Ana, California, and loves to create, stay fit, and play music. Visit *www.crescendoh.com*.